To God Be the Glory

TO GOD BE THE GLORY

Celebrating Twenty Years of Prison Fellowship Ministries

TYNDALE HOUSE PUBLISHERS, INC. WHEATON, ILLINOIS

All articles © by Prison Fellowship Ministries, previously published in their newsletter, *Jubilee.*
"Mel Goebel: A Clean Slate," "Lives Restored" © 1987 Prison Fellowship Ministries
"The Centrality of Christ," "When the Good Life Gives Out" © 1988 Prison Fellowship Ministries
"Eyes that See, Hands that Help," "Extending God's Arms" © 1989 Prison Fellowship Ministries
"Manny Makes the Grade," "Out of Season," "Countdown to Paradise" © 1990 Prison Fellowship Ministries
"Pennsylvania Lifeline," "The Fall and Rise of Charlie Cowart" © 1991 Prison Fellowship Ministries
"Praises, Prayers, and Promises," "Thirteen Years of Ministry," "Angel Tree Delivers" © 1993 Prison Fellowship Ministries
"Sharing Water from the Well," "Facing AIDS" © 1994 Prison Fellowship Ministries
"Serious Business" © 1995 Prison Fellowship Ministries

All photographs by David Singer, with the following exceptions: John Shaw: 39, 54, 70, 79, 81 (both), 83, 84, 89; John Meyer: 123, 124, 127;
David DeJong: 138 (both), 139; Benjamin Ragland, art contest winner: 56 (bottom right); Dean Felton, art contest winner: 56 (bottom left);
Barry Staver: 34 (left); Janice Fullman: 86 (right); Russ Busby: 55; Ben Baxter: 32; Unknown: x, 33, 34

PFM Coordinating Editor: Jan Kary
And with great appreciation to the following for their participation in this project:
Alan Terwilleger: Senior V.P., Ministry Advancement
David Carlson, Becky Beane, Peter Gross, John Shaw, Donna Varnam, Debra MacLean, Mark Mechler, Amy Philadelphia, Kevin Raleigh

Prison Fellowship Ministries thanks our very special partners in ministry at Tyndale House Publishers for their labor of love in creating this book:
Tammy Faxel, Special Sales Director   Andrea Gjeldum, Art Director/Designer   Nancy Buffenmyer, Production Coordinator
Sarah Peterson, Special Sales Editor   Paul Christenson, Assistant Designer/Keyliner
Kellye Strating, Special Sales Administrator   Christina Fox, Buyer

ISBN 0-8423-7181-8
Printed in Mexico.

00 99 98 97 96
 6   5   4   3   2   1

CONTENTS

In the eyes of the world, Charles W. Colson had it all: a beautiful wife, intelligent children, a successful law practice, and an appointment as President Nixon's special counsel. But something was missing.

As Watergate–related crimes began crashing down upon Chuck's "ideal" life, he realized that his worldly success hadn't gotten him anywhere. He was hopeless, empty.

Chuck's friend Tom Phillips had been feeling the same way—empty. As president of a large, profitable company at the age of forty, he defined the American Dream. But behind the material wealth, Tom knew there was an emptiness in his life. Says Tom, "It may be hard to understand, but I didn't seem to have anything that mattered. It was all on the surface. All the material things in life are meaningless if a man hasn't discovered what's underneath them." Tom searched for the answer. "I began to read the Scriptures, looking for answers. Something made me realize I needed a personal relationship with God and forced me to search." His search led him to a personal relationship with Jesus Christ.

After seeing the drastic change in his friend's life, Chuck questioned Tom about what had caused his new attitude of joy. The answer? Jesus Christ.

After reading MERE CHRISTIANITY by C. S. Lewis and recognizing the sin and emptiness that filled his life, Charles Colson gave his life to Christ. Although the road before him was uncertain, Chuck knew that he was no longer facing the future alone.

Colson served seven months at Maxwell Federal Prison Camp in Alabama for his Watergate-related crimes. From working as a laundry man to feeling the isolated loneliness, Colson lived the life of a typical prisoner. The only joy Chuck experienced was that which came from his relationship with Christ.

After his release, Colson vowed he would never return to a place like that . . . but he was haunted by the memory of a fellow inmate named Archie. In Colson's own words:

"I'd wake up in the middle of the night, that first week I was home from prison, thinking about one guy in particular, one black brother by the name of Archie.

"I WAS IN PRISON, AND YOU VISITED ME."

"One night when I was in prison, I was sitting in a dayroom in the dormitory. A lot of guys were crowded around the television and playing cards, and I was writing a letter home to Patty.

"Archie stood up with a deck of cards and said, 'Hey, Colson.' The place got quiet, and he said, 'What are you going to do for us, Colson, when you get out of here?'

"I said, 'Archie, I'll never forget guys like you.'

"And he took the cards and he said, 'Ah, bull! Big shots like you—you come into prison, and you get out, and then you forget little guys like me.'"

But Colson didn't forget, and in 1976 he and a small band of dedicated Christians launched Prison Fellowship Ministries, now the largest prison ministry in the world, to bring the good news of Jesus Christ to prisoners.

Just as the memory of Archie helped draw Chuck back to prison, another prisoner helped get Prison Fellowship off the ground.

After exhausting his political connections in an effort to start Prison Fellowship, Chuck knew he needed the backing of Norman Carlson, the no-nonsense director of the Federal Bureau of Prisons. As they met, Chuck carefully spelled out the failure of prisons to rehabilitate, the need to bring Jesus Christ to heal inmates' lives, and his desire to bring selected prisoners out of prison for Christian training. Carlson agreed—but not because of Chuck's persuasive discourse. It was the memory of a recent prison chapel service he had attended, where a prisoner in the back of the room prayed out loud for Carlson and his wife.

God used that prayer to touch the correctional official's heart—and opened the door for PFM to launch the Washington Discipleship Seminars. Inmates were furloughed for two weeks of Bible teaching and leadership training, then challenged

PARTICIPANTS IN THE FIRST WASHINGTON DISCIPLESHIP PROGRAM, BEGUN IN 1976.

to serve Christ upon returning to prison. Each year the program reached only fifty or so prisoners from federal institutions, but while Chuck and Prison Fellowship were trying to keep it going, God was preparing a new challenge.

In 1977 God again moved dramatically when a stubborn prison warden refused to furlough his prisoners to attend a PFM seminar. "If you guys are so good," the warden challenged Chuck, "why don't you bring your teaching into the prison?" Chuck accepted the challenge—and the first In-Prison Seminar was born.

Through that one stubborn warden, God charted a new direction for Prison Fellowship that Chuck had never imagined. The In-Prison Seminars soon became the backbone of PFM's ministry, bringing the gospel message to hundreds of thousands of prisoners throughout the U.S. During fiscal year 1994–1995, more than twenty-one hundred seminars drew a total inmate attendance of seventy thousand.

While seminars presented solid Christian teaching, they also provided a critical link between prisoners and local volunteers, making it possible for PFM to begin ongoing Bible studies inside the prisons. Today, more than 26,500 inmates meet in groups regularly to learn God's Word.

In 1983 PFM volunteer Mary Kay Beard recalled how many lonely Christmases she had spent in prison, separated from friends and family. Along with other interested volunteers, she launched Angel Tree®, a ministry to provide Christmas gifts for prisoners' children. That first year, God touched people's hearts to provide gifts for 556 children in

Alabama. In 1995 Angel Tree reached 463,000 children, opening up opportunities for year-round ministry to prisoners' families.

Through these core programs, PFM touched about 20 percent of the whole prison population. With the production of its prisoner newspaper, INSIDE JOURNAL, PFM's influence was extended to even more prisons, reaching an estimated five hundred thousand prisoners. But in 1992 a huge challenge still remained: How could PFM reach the vast 80 percent of prisoners who never went to anything that sounded religious?

Again, God moved dramatically—this time through a man named Aaron Johnson, then secretary of corrections for the state of North Carolina. Johnson opened up every prison door in his state to Prison Fellowship—more than ninety facilities—and invited the organization to saturate the prison system with the gospel message. To try to reach that elusive 80 percent, PFM launched the Starting Line, bringing in Christian athletes, musicians, and other entertainers for highly publicized in-prison events. In a two-week series of events, 75 percent of the prisoners showed up to hear the gospel, and after seeing the results, officials of four other states rushed to invite The Starting Line into their prisons. There seems to be no doubt that God is giving Prison Fellowship Ministries an expanded mission.

In countless ways God has moved miraculously to expand Prison Fellowship's impact on the lives of prisoners, ex-prisoners, and their families.

Through Justice Fellowship, begun in 1983, task force volunteers work for biblically based reforms in the criminal justice system. Through Neighbors Who Care, volunteers reach out to give help and encouragement to victims of crime.

Other Prison Fellowship volunteer ministries include mentoring, where volunteers support and help the ex-prisoner adjust to life outside prison. Mail Call matches prisoners with volunteer pen pals. Through Community Service Projects, furloughed prisoners preparing for parole work alongside volunteers to rejuvenate communities infested by crime. In MatchPoint, adult mentors work with youths in trouble, helping divert them from a path toward prison.

Along with the call to prison ministry, God has also given Chuck a growing burden to address the moral and spiritual barrenness of our culture—particularly its insidious infiltration of the church. Through his many books, speaking engagements, and his daily BreakPoint *radio commentary, Chuck boldly confronts current issues and values from a biblical perspective.*

In addition to ministering to prisoners in America, Prison Fellowship International serves in more than seventy chartered member countries around the world, reaching out to prisoners in foreign lands.

For the past twenty years Prison Fellowship has been fulfilling its mission to equip the church of Jesus Christ in its outreach to prisoners, ex-prisoners, crime victims, and their families, and to advance biblical standards of justice. As you read through To God Be the Glory: Celebrating Twenty Years of Prison Fellowship Ministries, *you will meet people whose lives have been radically transformed through PFM.*

———————————

IN MY SPIRIT I KNOW THERE'S ONE PLACE I WANT TO BE, AND THAT'S ON THE FRONT LINES, WHERE THE CUTTING EDGE OF THE GOSPEL IS BEING PROCLAIMED IN THE DARKEST PLACES OF THE WORLD. THAT IS THIS MOVEMENT IN THE PRISONS. I REALLY BELIEVE THAT THIS MOVEMENT HAS ONE OF THE GREATEST OPPORTUNITIES TO BE A WITNESS FOR THE KINGDOM OF GOD, TO SHOW THE WORLD PEACE, RIGHTEOUSNESS, AND THE JOY IN THE HOLY SPIRIT, WHICH ARE THE SIGNS OF THE KINGDOM TO COME.

CHARLES W. COLSON

CHUCK COLSON WITH AARON JOHNSON, THE FORMER SECRETARY OF CORRECTIONS OF NORTH CAROLINA, WHO OPENED UP EVERY PRISON IN THE STATE TO THE MINISTRIES OF PFM.

I | Eyes on the Savior

WHAT CAN HEAL A CRIMINAL'S HEART—EDUCATION, A GOOD JOB,

SOCIAL PROGRAMS? AS MUCH AS OUR CULTURE TRIES TO TELL US

OTHERWISE, CHRISTIANS KNOW THAT THE ONLY WAY TO TRUE

FREEDOM IS THROUGH A RELATIONSHIP WITH JESUS CHRIST.

EYES THAT SEE, HANDS THAT HELP

Ex-Inmate Miree Tolbert Brings Birmingham Prisoners Home

Out of prison only a few hours, a young man steps off a Greyhound bus into the stifling Birmingham heat. His eyes scan the transient crowd to see if he can pick out Miree Tolbert, a man he knows only through a couple of letters they've exchanged in past months.

Miree has no trouble spotting his man. In the last few years as a Prison Fellowship Aftercare coordinator and executive director of a home for ex-prisoners, he's picked up dozens of just-released inmates.

At last the ex-prisoner sees a serious-looking, middle-aged man pressing through the crowd toward him. As they shake hands, the man thinks Miree's large, deep brown eyes can see right through him.

In a way, they can. An ex-prisoner himself, Miree knows how frightening freedom can be after years of regimented living behind bars.

"I talk a lot when I pick a guy up," says Miree. "He's nearly in shock—has no plans for succeeding—and the talking comforts him."

Several hours later, after several stops around town, the ex-prisoner has three new sets of clothes, an ID card with photograph, and a gift pack of toiletries from Miree's home church, Christ Episcopal. Finally, Miree heads his '78 Dodge station wagon toward Shepherd's Fold.

The twenty-room, whitewashed two-story sits sleepily in the southwest section of Birmingham. At any given time, ten or more ex-prisoners live there as a family. Except for its distinctive parade of residents, the home resembles most others on the past-its-prime inner-city block.

For Miree, the journey to Shepherd's Fold has been much longer than a trip across town. In 1983 Miree lived in the

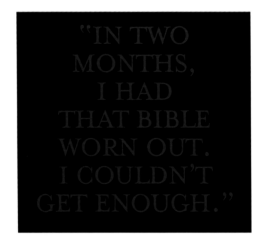

"IN TWO MONTHS, I HAD THAT BIBLE WORN OUT. I COULDN'T GET ENOUGH."

mountains of southern California, near Fresno, as part of a drug-smuggling ring so big that 200 conspirators were eventually arrested. Miree was one of them.

"A guy walked up to me on the second day of my stay at the Fresno County Jail and said, 'Man, you need to start reading the Bible,'" Miree recalls. Though he could read out of only one eye because of a serious infection, Miree asked the chaplain for a Bible. "In two months, I had

that Bible worn out," he says. "I couldn't get enough. One day I realized I was on my way to hell. I fell down on my face and asked the Lord to come into my life."

Miree was soon reading ten and twelve hours a day. During the next year at the Fresno jail, Miree began leading prayer groups and Bible studies. He prodded his fellow prisoners to attend Sunday worship services, where many received Christ. "They called me 'Preacher Man,'" he says.

Impressed by Miree's sincerity and quiet wisdom, the chaplain began spending an hour a day with him. The most memorable session came the day Miree finally got sentenced to the U.S. penitentiary in Lompoc for five years.

"See that picture on my desk?" asked the chaplain. The photograph was wrinkled, but Miree recognized the familiar face in a surprising setting. The man was being released from prison.

"That's me thirty years ago," the chaplain continued. "I've been doing for you what somebody else did for me. Always remember that to whom much is given, much is required!"

The Preacher Man never forgot the chaplain's challenge. He remained obedient to the Lord as he mentally tallied the months of his sentence, first at Lompoc, then at Maxwell Federal Prison Camp in his native Alabama.

I'VE HAD TO BE AS WISE AS A SERPENT AND GENTLE AS A DOVE," SAYS EX-PRISONER MIREE TOLBERT OF HIS ROLES AS PFM'S AFTERCARE COORDINATOR AND NOW AS THE ALABAMA AREA DIRECTOR.

Then four years ago, released before his sentence was up, Miree sat on the passenger's side of a ride to Shepherd's Fold. In the driver's seat was Don Beard, founder and former executive director of the home. Don's wife, Mary Kay, then served as PFM area director for Alabama. After hosting Miree during a Community Service Project, they'd asked him to come be a live-in counselor at the home they'd renovated and opened to ex-prisoners.

"Out of prison, the first thing I learned was to establish an accountability relationship with another person," says Miree. "For me that was Don. The second person to spend lots of time with me was the new Alabama PFM area director, Steve Longenecker, after Don and Mary Kay relocated to Texas."

Before moving, the Beards asked Miree to become executive director of Shepherd's Fold. After a month of praying—and living away from the home to get some perspective—he accepted in September 1987.

Miree still has to do lots of praying. First, there are the finances to keep straight. Dependent totally upon charitable donations, Miree must raise funds, pay bills, buy food, fix leaky sinks, repair the car—the list goes on, even when the money doesn't.

More important, there are lives to keep straight. Under his guidance, residents must look for work, do house chores, be present at evening meals and Bible study, and attend a biblically sound church on Sundays. "Each guy must also commit to a mentoring relationship," says Miree, "where there's an ongoing accountability exchange."

Miree estimates that fifty to seventy-five guys pass through Shepherd's Fold each

"MY JOB IS TO BE FAITHFUL —TO PLANT AND TO WATER."

year. By the time a guy leaves, usually after a six- to twelve-month stay, Miree hopes he will have a stable job, a solid relationship with the Lord, and a savings account of at least $1,000. PFM's monthly ex-offender support group that Miree helped start focuses on such goals.

Miree, however, has no illusions about expecting perfection. "My job is to be faithful—to plant and to water," he says. "If you go into ministry with a success mind-set, you are barking up the wrong tree."

During his early days as director, Miree also learned that he couldn't do it by himself. "I had to plug my guys into the resource bank of Aftercare," he says, referring to PFM volunteers, other spiritually strong ex-prisoners, and nearly a dozen nearby churches.

But like the shepherd of the New Testament parable, Miree often leaves the comfort of his fold to find one of his misguided sheep. If a guy loses a job, Miree spends time with him, patching the wounded pride. If a guy violates house rules, Miree takes him for a ride and talks things over, pointing the guy on the right road.

"I do most of my counseling in this car," says Miree.

Miree's post is not easy, nor his compassion cheap. His brow wrinkles when he hears a guy didn't make it in by curfew. *Hope it's not drugs.* At the news of a guy who's had to return to prison, the crease deepens. *No, God, not him. He was so strong.*

But Miree can't quit caring. Ninety-nine out of a hundred may be safely tucked away, but the cry of the guy who's lost won't leave Miree any peace. He knows that one day, not so many years ago, that cry was his. He's glad somebody answered.

JANE [WILLIS] GARDNER
From the September 1989 issue of JUBILEE

SIX PERCENT OF
ALL PRISONERS
ARE WOMEN.

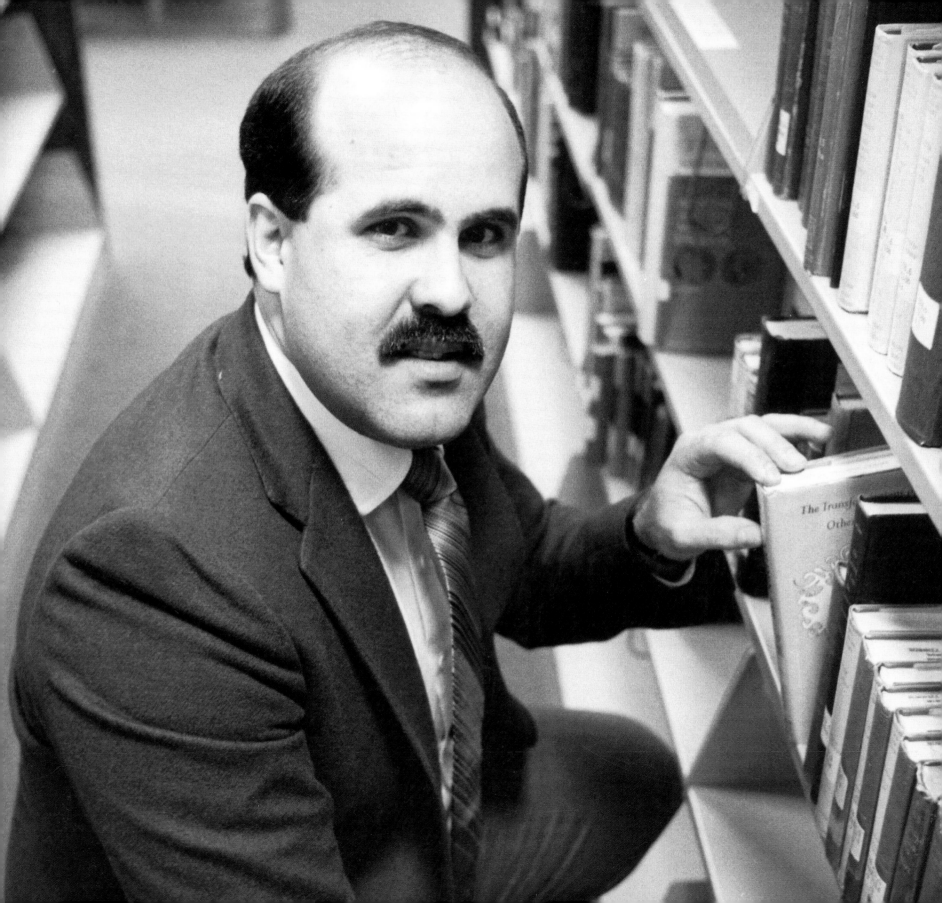

Meet Manny Mill, Big Man on Campus. As he walks spiritedly across the grounds at Wheaton College, it seems everyone knows him: professors, students, and staff. Manny has an encouraging word to share with everyone he meets.

He's smooth with the books, too. All A's and B's. Having just completed his bachelor's degree, he's tackling a master's in theology.

There are several things that distinguish Manny from the other nearly twenty-two hundred students at this nondenominational, evangelical school near Chicago: his charismatic personality, his high energy level, his Hispanic heritage, his age (he's thirty-three) . . . his prison record.

Manny is a recipient of the Charles W. Colson Scholarship, awarded to ex-prisoners who attend Wheaton.

One by one, Manny is meeting the requirements necessary for him to return to the federal prison system—this time as a chaplain, emphasizing ministry to Hispanics.

Manuel Mill, born in Cuba, spent his teenage years on the move with his parents and sisters: from Spain to Atlanta to New Jersey, where he settled in Union City.

Manny was, in his words, "very active" in New Jersey: as an aide to the mayor, as the city's director of neighborhood preservation, as a full-time student at Seton Hall University, where he played baseball. On the side, he promoted Hispanic shows, dances, and cruises.

Eventually Manny became one of the top salesmen in the country for Prudential Insurance. "I was making so much money, I said, 'Who needs college?' and dropped out." Subsequently, when a competing firm offered him a better deal in Miami,

> "I WAS MAKING SO MUCH MONEY, I SAID, 'WHO NEEDS COLLEGE?' AND DROPPED OUT."

he headed south.

"The dream of every Cuban is to move to Miami," says Manny. "I saw this as a great opportunity. I even opened my own agency."

Then it struck.

"Greed. I had a beautiful home, three cars, a thriving agency, a family. And this guy comes to me and says I can make $50,000 easy. I was blind [to the crime].

I just saw the money."

Manny's role was to find a Florida banker to cash three forged New Jersey checks totaling $175,000. Crossing state lines with bad paper is a federal offense. Enter the FBI, for whom the banker sang "Manny's Song." Not wishing to trade his pinstripes for prison stripes, Manny packed up his wife and son and skipped the country, landing in Puerto Rico, the Dominican Republic, and Colombia before settling in Venezuela.

"I was in Caracas for twenty-one months," Manny says. "I opened a restaurant and was doing well. Gained twenty pounds."

Manny was in no hurry to head north, until he received a phone call from his father in January 1986. "I hadn't talked to my dad since I'd left Miami," says Manny. "I couldn't face him. He'd had high hopes for me, and I had disappointed him."

Though Manny didn't know it, the FBI had asked his father to convince him to come home. Manny was not prepared for his father's question: "If I die tonight, will you be able to come to my wake?"

Manny hated to disillusion his father any further, but he spoke the truth. "No, Dad. The FBI is looking for me."

"I know," his father answered. "I know how many counts you have. I know how much time you're facing."

"Something happened to me that I cannot explain," Manny recalls. "I felt two inches tall. Tears came to my eyes. 'Dad, I have failed you. I have failed Mom. I have failed everybody.'"

Manny's mom, a Christian since 1978, was also on the line.

"Manny," she said, "you need to fix your life now. You need to have the courage and the guts to face what you've done.

"You're not really running from those people; you're running from God . . . from sin . . . like Jonah. No one can hide from God."

His mother's words struck home. Manny says, "I began to weep and repent for what I had done, not only to my family but to God. Then I realized the mess I had made of my life."

Manny gathered his family and surrendered to FBI agents on February 12, 1986, at Kennedy Airport. Five months later he began serving a thirty-six-month sentence at the federal prison camp in Allenwood, Pennsylvania.

Prison life did not slow down Manny.

His first order of business was to start a morning prayer meeting. Three men—eventually fifty—met on weekdays before going to work. He added another meeting at the beginning of the night shift.

Manny discovered Prison Fellowship —and vice versa—through volunteer Gordon

Barnes, who arrived at Allenwood shortly after Manny. A corrections officer at Mercer County Jail, Gordon, and his wife, Diane, led a weekly PFM Bible study and assisted at In-Prison Seminars. Manny helped promote PFM activities and led a weekly Hispanic Bible study.

After ten months in prison, it was put-up-or-shut-up time for Manny and his

> "YOU'RE NOT REALLY RUNNING FROM THOSE PEOPLE; YOU'RE RUNNING FROM GOD."

Christianity: His wife of nine years divorced him (and subsequently remarried). "I felt terrible," says Manny. "But I had Christ. I had counseled inmates in similar situations. Now I had to put into practice the principles I had been telling them to hold on to."

His hope of returning to his family shattered, Manny began to question his future, his role in God's kingdom.

"I prayed, 'God, I want to be who You

want me to be. I need You to show me what You want me to do when I leave here.'"

Manny felt the Lord wanted him to return to college, and he shared this dream with Chaplain Manuel Cordero, who knew no way around the major obstacles: the cost of tuition and the fact that most colleges would not consider an ex-prisoner until he had been out for at least a year. "Let's wait to see what God has to say about this," said the chaplain.

A few weeks later the chaplain received a letter from Don Smarto, director of Wheaton's Institute for Prison Ministries, announcing a new scholarship bearing Chuck Colson's name. In faith, Manny sent in an application, even though he had nearly two years to go on his sentence.

About a month later Manny was selected to attend PFM's Washington Discipleship Seminar, scheduled for January 1988. At first, counselors at Allenwood refused Manny furlough, considering it a risk because of his flight to Venezuela. But when those staff members were transferred, Manny got the go-ahead—two days before he was to leave for Washington.

At a banquet near the end of the seminar, Manny sat next to a stranger, PFM board member Ken Wessner. Manny remembers the conversation: "What are you going to do when you leave prison?"

"Well, I'm going by faith to Wheaton College." The conversation picked up, and Wessner, formerly chairman of the board at Wheaton, became one of many people who would recommend Manny for a Colson scholarship.

Manny returned to Allenwood to discover that a change of law had reduced his sentence. Released on April 6, Manny enrolled at Wheaton on July 5. Once classwork began, Manny discovered what studying was all about. "It has been tough, but I have adjusted," he says.

And, of course, there were ministries to begin.

Manny started a "basket" prayer ministry in his dormitory. "People would come to the dormitory and put their prayer requests in a basket in the lounge," says Manny. "Guys would come to my room every night to pray about these requests. But the room got too small and the basket too full." So Manny spoke to the college chaplain, and the basket was moved to the chapel. "Then it became a ministry for the whole campus."

Manny acquired a reputation among the students; they would schedule time—especially at meals—to talk. "I was booked for the whole month to eat with guys and ladies just for counseling."

After nearly two years, Manny has more than settled in.

"I feel that this is my home," he says. "This environment has changed my life. It has given me the opportunity to broaden my horizons. College even gave me the chance to meet my wife."

Barbara Mills is Manny's beautiful wife. Husband and wife since January 6, they met last July [1989] in Jerusalem.

By a "miracle of God," Manny was allowed to leave the U.S. while still on parole to study abroad at the Institute of Holy Land Studies. Barbara was there with a group of students from Philadelphia College of Bible, where she was on staff. Manny and Barbara met on July 13, the day his parole expired.

"My wife has been an instrument from God to put brakes on me," says Manny. "I'm a train that won't stop. When I go, I go. My wife has been able to say, 'Stop and think.'

"People who are in jail did not stop and think. I was in prison with many doctors, lawyers, and accountants. Why did they trade years of school for years of suffering? Greed and sin. People make mistakes because they don't think about the consequences. If people would stop, pray, and think, they would be less likely to make a mistake. I have learned that."

NATE BROWN
From the May 1990 issue of JUBILEE

LONELINESS CAN EAT
AWAY AT THE HEART
OF A PRISONER.

SMALL-GROUP BIBLE
STUDIES ENCOURAGE
INMATES TO
DIG DEEPER INTO
THE TRUTHS OF
SCRIPTURE.

The applause faded, and the women participating in a Prison Fellowship In-Prison Seminar broke into discussion groups.

Several inmates had just acted out the story of Jesus' encounter with the Samaritan woman, an outcast, a sinner. As a small-group leader, volunteer Ann Bonham posed a question: "If you had been the woman at the well, how would you have reacted to Jesus?"

One woman glared knives at Ann. "It doesn't matter how I would have felt, or anybody else," she snapped. "You don't know what it's like to be in prison!"

Unruffled, Ann leaned toward her accuser. "Honey, I'm sorry. I don't know how you feel," she said gently. "But I know how *I* felt before I left these gates."

The stare softened. "Then teach us," the woman replied. Thirsty for the Living Water, she committed her life to Christ the next day.

"God restores sinners and quenches dry spirits, but first He has to get your attention," says Ann. "And sometimes He has to put you in prison to do that. That's what it took for me."

According to Ann, her wayward journey started in high school, when she recognized Christ as her Savior but didn't "walk the talk." Reared under the white-gloved thumb of an army-colonel father, she bucked the regimentation and control. "I was determined to do things my own way," she says, which included marrying Cliff a few years out of high school despite warning signs of his alcoholism. "I thought I could change him," she explains.

But when she couldn't change him, she started to blame him for their growing financial problems. In reality, the more he spent on whiskey, the more she sought revenge by going on shopping binges.

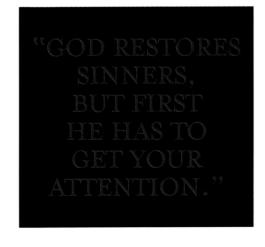

"GOD RESTORES SINNERS, BUT FIRST HE HAS TO GET YOUR ATTENTION."

As a bank employee, Ann resorted to creative accounting schemes—her perceived ticket out of impending financial wreckage. Over two years she routed $13,000 into her own account, all the while growing more and more tense in trying to hide her activities. Getting caught "was really a relief," she admits.

But Cliff felt differently. In May 1986, as Ann headed from their Midland, Texas, home for the Correctional Institution in Fort Worth, Cliff told her to "be prepared for divorce papers." And their two daughters would go with him.

But Cliff's firm conviction that "marriage is forever" was rooted deeper than his anger and hurt. A month later he climbed on his motorcycle and faced 200 miles of wind to deliver a different message: "We're going to work this out."

Cliff's devotion cracked Ann's steadfast refusal to take responsibility for her crime. "It's not all Cliff's fault," she finally admitted. "It's time to change Ann, too."

When Ann got out of prison in four months, things went well at first; Cliff was even drinking less. But when Cliff's work moved the family to North Carolina, Ann's new parole officer triggered memories of her regimented childhood. "So I rebelled," she says. "I wouldn't send in my reports or pay my restitution."

Facing another prison term for violating parole and depressed that Cliff was drinking again, Ann saw only one way out. At home alone one afternoon, Ann slashed her wrists and waited to die.

But she hadn't counted on a fortuitous intervention. A police officer had called Cliff at work asking where Ann was; her car was in the driveway, but no one answered the door. The officer wanted to talk to her about some money missing from Ann's place of employment. Cliff went home to check on Ann and rushed

In 1991 Ann walked out of North Carolina's Fountain Correctional Center. Today she and her husband, Cliff, go back to share the freedom they've found in Christ.

NO WEAPONS BEYOND THIS POINT

Once threatening divorce, Cliff chose instead to stick with his imprisoned wife. Now they are partners in ministry as well as in marriage.

to bandage her self-inflicted gashes.

Later, at the police station, Ann insisted she had nothing to do with the alleged theft. "But I was tired; I had lost a lot of blood. And finally I said, 'Get it over with. Just charge me.'"

Several weeks later she was back in prison, where God abruptly grabbed her attention. Her new roommate greeted her with a Bible and a warning: "You're not going to make it, and you're not going to get right unless you get *this* right, too."

With no TV or radio and no one to talk to while her roommate studied her Bible, "What else was there for me to do but to read the Bible too?" she said.

Meanwhile, God also grabbed Cliff's attention through a friend who persistently invited him to Grace Covenant Church, where he committed his life to Christ.

Outside the prison and in, the Bonhams started to "walk the talk." Ann continued to fill her mind with Scripture, its "two-edged sword" shaving off the jagged edges of rebellion and carving out a love for her fellow inmates. Prison Fellowship volunteers encouraged the Bonhams, particularly through Angel Tree, providing Christmas gifts for their daughter Connie.

In early 1990 Ann was transferred to North Carolina to serve out her last sentence for theft—and to learn new lessons about Jesus and His love for others.

"At first I didn't want to associate with them," says Ann—"them" being drug abusers, murderers, lesbians. "I thought I was going to find somebody 'like me.' But then I realized that that was all of us; we were all just a number there. So I started talking to them, getting to know them. And after a while, I could feel myself wanting to give more.

"When you meet somebody who has murdered a child, how do you relate? When you walk into the bathroom and somebody is shooting up, how are you going to react? You've got to let God work in you to reach out. That same one who killed her baby may be having a hard day. Are you going to just let her sit there by herself, or are you going to take the love of God to her?"

Released from Fountain Correctional Center two years later, Ann immediately signed up for training to join Cliff in his volunteer work with Prison Fellowship.

Today the Bonhams teach PFM seminars in prisons across North Carolina. But the trips back to Fountain inspire Ann the most—back to the "Samaritan" women who once shared her dorm room and cafeteria tables.

At one seminar Ann asked participants to volunteer to read parts in a skit. "Me! Me!" one woman shouted, waving her hand. Ann hesitated; while incarcerated she had tried to teach this prisoner to read. "But she barely got past *a, an,* and *the,*" Ann recalls. Against her better judgment, she handed the inmate a script.

She read like a champ. At the end of the skit, she turned to her former tutor, now in tears. "This is for Ann. Because you encouraged me, I got my GED" (a high school equivalency diploma).

Ann also gives a helping hand to newly released inmates—like Sarah, a former addict now drug free and living on her own. Employed as a social worker with the Salvation Army, Ann helped Sarah secure food, furniture, and funds for her rent. And she regularly calls with an encouraging word or an offer to drive Sarah to church.

Not every person the Bonhams touch is a success story. "You plant seeds; that's all you can do," says Ann. "I am not the judge of others. I don't have to answer for their actions. But I have to answer for not loving them.

"It's those few you *do* touch" that make Ann's joy overflow like a fountain. "Because you know that each one"—like the Samaritan woman—"will in turn touch somebody else."

BECKY BEANE
From the June 1994 issue of JUBILEE

MEL GOEBEL: A CLEAN SLATE

Omaha, Nebraska, February 1971. "The court finds Melvin R. Goebel guilty on one count of burglary. He is sentenced to two to five years of hard labor at the Nebraska State Penitentiary."

Two years later twenty-two-year-old Mel Goebel sat in the asphalt yard of Lincoln Correctional Center (LCC). He stared at the concrete walls and razor wire, thinking of ways to smuggle in pot, the drug that had helped him drift through this incarceration. His thoughts were interrupted when a bus full of new prisoners—mostly uninitiated kids—arrived and started to unload.

Mel's eyes focused on a guy in a khaki jacket with black lettering on the back: "Smile, Jesus is your Friend."

Is that guy nuts? he thought. *The guys are going to tear him apart.*

Mel sauntered up to the kid and pulled him aside. "Tell me about this Jesus." There was a sneer in his voice. "I've never seen any love in people."

The new guy was silent for a moment, then he said, "Christ will give you peace of mind. He'll give you direction and overflow your life with joy and happiness."

That night Mel pondered the young man's words. He remembered the Jesus of his childhood. Could this Jesus be real?

The question wouldn't leave. After a few days he sought out Fred, the khaki-jacketed prisoner. "What about the suffering in the world?" he asked. "How come I've had to go through all this pain?"

"It's a walk of faith," Fred replied, opening his Bible. "You have to read the Holy Scriptures and come to grips with these questions yourself." Mel returned to his cell to think; later he borrowed a Bible from the chapel, and the words he read— of love and forgiveness—penetrated deeply.

One day Mel returned from work duty early. He knelt in the cell's curtained toilet area, tears rolling down his cheeks,

> HE KNELT IN THE CELL'S CURTAINED TOILET AREA, TEARS ROLLING DOWN HIS CHEEKS, AND CONFESSED HIS SIN.

and confessed his sin. That day he found God's forgiveness—and the peace he'd been looking for.

Being a Christian changed Mel's outlook on prison. Before, he was consumed with thoughts about getting out. Now, he learned to be content. He viewed prison as a monastery where he could study the Bible, form close friendships, and practice his Christianity.

News of his conversion spread quickly.

One of his friends with whom Mel used to get high was in solitary confinement when Mel accepted the Lord. When Rick returned to the general population, he sought out Mel. Rick was angry, fearing that he had lost a friend, and he doubted Mel's sincerity.

Mel told Rick how Jesus had brought him forgiveness, and showed him passages in the Bible. That afternoon, Rick committed his life to the Lord.

About a year later, an eighteen-year-old inmate named Rocky came to Mel's cell. He, too, had heard about Mel's conversion. With tears in his eyes, the boy explained his story: When he first came to prison, he had accepted a carton of pot and some cigarettes from older inmates. Now the "goon squad" wanted to collect payment in homosexual "favors."

Not sure what to do, Mel and some other Christians scraped together their change and bought a carton of cigarettes at the commissary. Then Mel walked alone to the gym where the inmates—his old gang—waited. Right away he spotted Eric, the tall, muscular man who had once been his leader.

"It was the first time my faith was on the line," Mel says. "When I saw those four guys standing there, I realized that since coming to Christ, I'd forgotten the prison code of toughness."

PF Board Member Dallen Peterson (left) has been Mel's friend for many years, first as a Bible study leader in the prison, then as a mentor on the outside.

Believing in the importance of personal development, Mel Goebel obtained a degree in organizational communication from University of Nebraska, Omaha.

Janes' quiet, constant support has been invaluable to Mel during their seventeen years of marriage.

He walked to the back of the gym and held out the cigarettes. "Here's the carton Rocky owes you," he said. "I never collected the two cartons of pot you owed me, so the debt is canceled."

Eric stepped forward. "Who do you think you are, telling us what to do?"

Mel's heart beat hard, but he stood his ground. "Because of Christ, Rocky's my brother," he said, his voice shaking. "I have to help him." Expecting to be jumped, Mel turned and walked away. But no one followed.

Back in the yard, Mel told two other Christian inmates what had happened. As they talked, one of them looked up and saw Eric walking toward them. Seven or eight big guys surrounded him, swearing and encouraging him to beat up Mel.

The three Christians exchanged looks; what would Jesus have them do? "The servant is not greater than the master," one of them said. Jesus had been bruised and battered. If people had persecuted Him, they would persecute His followers, too.

Mel says, "We were prepared to take a beating for the Lord. After four years in prison, I knew people who would fight for me, but we decided against it. Even though I was afraid, I knew the Lord was with me."

When Eric was face-to-face with Mel, he scowled. "I don't think I like what you did down there." He moved closer.

Mel took a deep breath and looked his old leader in the eyes. "Eric, if you were being threatened, I would do the same thing for you."

The gang leader turned and walked away; he hadn't seen that kind of love before. Slowly, the others followed.

"That day," says Mel, "I learned that 1 John 4:4 holds true: 'Greater is he that is in you, than he that is in the world' (KJV). I also learned the importance of warning new inmates about prison traps." Subsequently, Mel and his brothers greeted the weekly busloads of inmates and told them about the Christian community at LCC.

When Mel was released in 1976, he left the company of one Christian fellowship but walked into the arms of a supportive group in Omaha.

At Calvary Lutheran Church, Mel met Jane Danischek, whom he married in 1979. Shortly after their wedding, Jane's father gave Mel a copy of *Jubilee*. Mel was impressed with what he saw. He contacted Prison Fellowship and attended a Washington Discipleship Seminar, where they saw evidence of his mature faith. A few months later, he joined PFM's staff as a state director. His compassion for people helped him nurture both volunteers and inmates.

In 1983, after helping Prison Fellowship get started in Colorado, Mel returned to Omaha to pursue a college degree. This was a big step for someone who had dropped out of eleventh grade because of a prison sentence. PFM kept Mel on staff part-time, so he continued to work with prisoners in Omaha.

One of Mel's greatest accomplishments was to start a support group for ex-offenders. Last December [1986] he stood in the Nebraska capitol building and appealed for a state pardon. He wanted his crime erased from the records so he could enjoy the full rights of a citizen. He explained that he had "paid his dues," then devoted his life to helping others.

As he awaited the verdict, Mel shifted in his seat. At last the governor arose and announced that Mel would receive a full pardon. The slate was washed clean. "Forgiveness is instant with God," says Mel, "but with society it takes much longer."

Referring to the hearing, Mel says, "It reminded me that someday we all are going to face God. If I was that nervous in a secular courtroom, how will people who are not confident of Jesus' forgiveness feel before the throne of God? Because I know that He can forgive, I need to tell others. For me, that calling is in prison."

ALICE LAWSON
SPERAPANI
From the May 1987 issue of JUBILEE

II | A LIFELINE OF LOVE

HOW DO VOLUNTEERS MAKE A DIFFERENCE? FROM BEFRIENDING A

LONELY PRISONER TO AIDING A VICTIM TO ADVOCATING IMPROVEMENTS

IN THE CRIMINAL JUSTICE SYSTEM, VOLUNTEERS BRING COMPASSION,

DEDICATION, AND GOOD NEWS TO THOSE WHO ARE HURTING.

Annie Howard spends too much time at Kentucky Correctional Institution for Women (KCIW) near Louisville. Or so the residents say. She's been warned: "We're going to get you a bed. You're here more than you're at home. We're just going to let you move in with us."

She doesn't spend that much time at KCIW, yet she's there twenty to fifty hours a month. Last year she even went in on Christmas Day. "It's difficult, but it's letting Jesus love through me. I'm just an extension of His arms."

But Annie doesn't minister alone. As the Prison Fellowship volunteer coordinator for Kentucky, Annie has established a network of volunteers from more than twenty-five churches to oversee a wide range of activities for KCIW residents.

Annie's initial involvement in prison ministry stemmed from a friend's asking her to start a Bible study at KCIW, where she delivered Gideon New Testaments. The chaplain gave her a green light in October 1979, and she's still leading that study every Tuesday night.

For the past year the Bible study has been followed by "praise, dance and drama," in which volunteer instructors help the residents act out prepared scripts of Bible stories. "The sessions are fun," says Annie, "and they give residents an opportunity to help one another in their personal growth.

"One resident had a particularly poor self-image and really couldn't read," Annie says. "But the women would rally around her. Someone would stand beside her and whisper all the words to her so she would be able to say her part."

Annie discovered Prison Fellowship in 1982 when the first of many seminars was held at the prison. Since then, she has

> ## "IT'S DIFFICULT, BUT IT'S LETTING JESUS LOVE THROUGH ME."

spearheaded an intensive training program for volunteers. She says, "When I would coordinate a seminar, I would always make sure that the volunteers understood the guidelines of the institution."

Those prison guidelines are instrumental in KCIW's One-to-One program, in which thirty-six residents are each matched with a specific woman or couple who visits them regularly.

"The residents have to request a volunteer," Annie says. "I do not match men with women, though I have three couples I have matched with a resident. I love having couples because that shows a family unit."

Annie urges volunteers and residents alike to build relationships without expecting something in return.

"That's very difficult for volunteers," she says, "because they naturally want to give materially. But the greatest thing you can give is yourself. And that's what we ask, that they give of themselves—their time, their love, their listening ear."

Building trust in the prisoners is an additional challenge for Annie. "Their whole life has been a disappointment. Then volunteers make commitments. It's hard for the residents to understand if they're not kept. One resident who has no family—no one—has a One-to-One visitor who lives out of the city and sometimes has car trouble. One day the resident said to me, 'She didn't come this week.' Then big tears came. I said, 'Well, I know there's a good reason. . . .'" With assurances Annie tried to soothe her crushed spirit.

Annie herself receives encouragement from inside and outside the institution. One guard, Annie says, always greets her with a smile or a hug. The corrections staff, including Warden Betty Kassulke, supports the PFM programs, as does Annie's home church, Southeast Christian.

To involve more churches in prison

ministry, Annie created a crafts program at KCIW. Twelve churches each commit to one Saturday night per year, she says. "They bring in ten to twenty volunteers who teach a craft project. The residents can take the completed crafts—baskets, paper earrings, painted T-shirts—back to their living areas."

What keeps Annie going? "The Holy Spirit never burns out," she says. "I know, without a doubt, that the Lord asked me to start this. There are a few times of discouragement, but I think of the love that I get back from the women because they see me there so much."

Annie's presence has left a lasting impression on the residents. Recently, as she passed by the infirmary of KCIW, she heard a meek voice: "Annie?"

Annie grasped for a name to match the face she remembered so well. Seven years earlier the woman had attended Annie's Tuesday night Bible study faithfully for a year, though she'd never said a word.

"It amazed me that she'd remembered my name," Annie says of the woman, paroled, then recommitted to KCIW. "At some point in their lives they can think back and know that somebody loved them. This resident was a confirmation of that. Just because I loved her, she remembered."

NATE BROWN

From the June 1989 issue of JUBILEE

KENTUCKY VOLUNTEER COORDINATOR ANNIE HOWARD HAS ESTABLISHED A NETWORK OF VOLUNTEERS FROM MORE THAN TWENTY-FIVE CHURCHES TO OVERSEE A VARIETY OF ACTIVITIES FOR KENTUCKY'S FEMALE PRISONERS.

BOXER MARVIS FRAZIER
(SON OF JOE FRAZIER)
SHARES THE JOY OF
CHRIST WITH THESE
INMATES.

JUST TWO WEEKS AFTER WINNING THE
SUPERBOWL IN 1992, REDSKINS' HEAD COACH,
JOE GIBBS, VISITED A WASHINGTON, D.C., PRISON
AND GAVE HIS TESTIMONY (FULL PAGE RIGHT).

THE STARTING LINE

The Starting Line is an innovative evangelistic campaign that saturates a state's prison population with the message of Christ's forgiveness and power. To draw out the nonchapel crowd, events feature highly talented Christian musicians and entertainers, dynamic athletes, and powerhouse speakers, who can attract even the most skeptical inmates and win an opening to explain the gospel. In the states that have already hosted Starting Line events, up to 80 percent of the prisoners have come out to hear the Good News.

What hooks them may be the celebrity show. But what helps open their hearts is the genuine Christian love expressed by the entertainers, speakers, and other volunteers. The realness of Christian faith shines through their songs, their words, and their actions.

NOW I AM SAVED, AND I WANT TO BE
STRONGER WITH IT. GOD WILL LEAD ME.
I AM NOT GOING TO TURN MY BACK
ON HIM NO MORE. I AM STRIVING FOR
THE BEST.
—*a prisoner who trusted Christ during The Starting Line*

I SAW A LOT OF MEN COME [TO THE
STARTING LINE EVENTS] WHO WOULD
NEVER, EVER SET FOOT INSIDE A
REGULAR CHURCH SERVICE.
—*prison program supervisor, North Carolina*

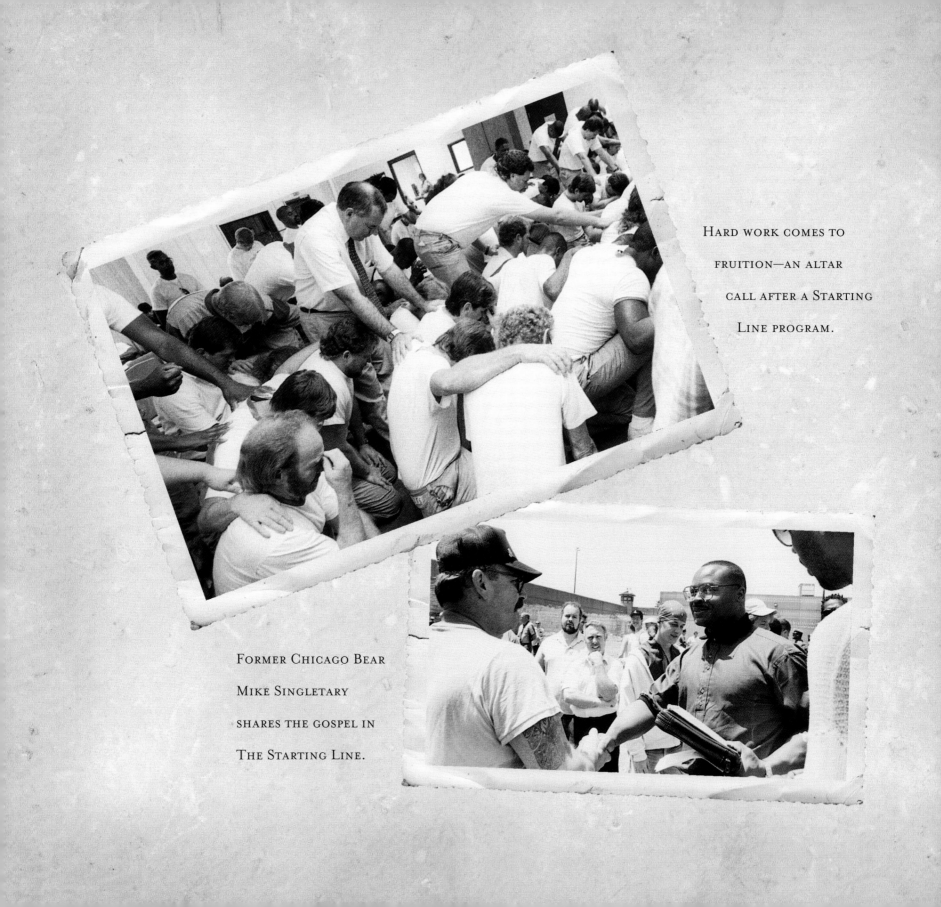

Hard work comes to fruition—an altar call after a Starting Line program.

Former Chicago Bear Mike Singletary shares the gospel in The Starting Line.

STEVEN CURTIS CHAPMAN SHARES HIS GIFT OF MUSIC WITH INMATES.

MAIL CALL MINISTRY

Through Mail Call, PFM matches interested prisoners with volunteer pen pals, whose letters bring warmth and care to a cold and lonely environment. More than seventeen thousand prisoners now correspond regularly with their PFM-matched pen pals.

Myrtie Howel, ninety-one years old but wanting to serve, wrote to twenty to thirty inmates through Mail Call. She has now passed away, leaving a legacy to many prison "grandchildren."

After she became a Christian, Pam Walton's priorities changed dramatically. Setting aside a successful career, she devotes nearly full time to ministries, including Neighbors Who Care, in Denver.

After completing fourteen hours of volunteer training, Pam received her first assignment: Take the love of Christ to a burglary victim. While another NWC volunteer replaced a broken window, Pam held the victim's hand and listened with an ear of compassion.

Pam's motivation is straightforward: "I have a call to serve Jesus Christ"—whom she sees in the eyes of the crime victims she calls and visits.

Neighbors Who Care—reaching out to those who have been victims of crime.

Justice Fellowship is the criminal justice reform arm of Prison Fellowship Ministries. Through various programs, JF pursues three strategic objectives:

1. Victims' Rights: To grant victims a formal role in the criminal justice process, including the right to participate in criminal cases and the right to restitution and reconciliation.

2. Intermediate Punishments: To sentence nonviolent offenders to community service, restitution, and other intermediate sanctions that hold offenders accountable and protect the public.

3. Prison Work Programs: To emphasize the need for a healthy, viable work program in every prison to the end that as many prisoners as possible be gainfully employed.

MANY PEOPLE COME HERE TO DO RELIGIOUS

SERVICES, BUT WE . . . APPRECIATE YOU

PRISON FELLOWSHIP VOLUNTEERS BECAUSE

YOU . . . TREAT US LIKE PEOPLE INSTEAD OF

PREACHING DOWN TO US AS OTHERS DO.

—a prisoner

III | A Guiding Hand

"PRISON FELLOWSHIP . . . COULD JUST POSSIBLY BE THE

AGENT OF THE MOST IMPORTANT PRISON REFORMS OF THE

CENTURY . . . COLSON'S CRUSADE IS PROFOUNDLY CONCEIVED,

EXISTENTIALLY APPEALING, SPLENDID IN AMBITION."

—WILLIAM F. BUCKLEY, JR.

It began like any Saturday morning. Patty and I usually allow ourselves an extra half hour of sleep on weekends. This day was bright, an April sun streaming through the French doors and into our bedroom.

I plodded to the bathroom, stared through sleepy-eyed fog into the mirror, and reached for the shaving cream. As I stared at my reflection, a startling series of pictures flashed across my mind. Men in prison gray moving about. Classes. Discussions. Prayers.

"Of course, of course," I whispered as if in response to obvious commands. "Take the prisoners out, teach them, return them to prisons to build Christian fellowships. Spread these fellowships through every penitentiary in America."

I was now wide awake, my heart racing, every nerve in my body alive and exhilarated. I can still remember how vivid and lifelike it was. Before my eyes was a simple plan with every detail fitting into place. More than thoughts, I saw sharply focused pictures—of smiling men and women streaming out of prisons, of Bibles and study groups, of fellowship around tables.

These mental images lasted but a few seconds, then they were gone. I had never experienced anything like this before or since.

Was it of God? Or just a flash of inspiration, like any good idea that pops suddenly into one's consciousness. Even as I splashed cold water on my face, I felt an unusual assurance. Excitedly, I dried my hands and face and raced to the telephone.

"Harold . . . this is Chuck. . . . Sorry to bother you, but can we get together?"

> AS I STARED AT MY REFLECTION, A STARTLING SERIES OF PICTURES FLASHED ACROSS MY MIND. MEN IN PRISON GRAY MOVING ABOUT. CLASSES. DISCUSSIONS. PRAYERS.

Twenty minutes later Harold Hughes was sipping coffee in my makeshift basement office. "Brother, you may think I'm crazy," I began. Then I outlined what had appeared to me.

As I spoke, the details became even more clear: The inmates would be furloughed out of prisons in twos, probably for two-week periods, maybe three. The principles of discipleship would be taught at Fellowship House; the prisoners could be quartered nearby.

Harold was intent, though I wondered if he thought I had eaten something too rich the night before. My words, as I heard them, were describing a very radical idea.

When I finished, Harold leaned back in his chair. "It's of God, no doubt about it." Then he heaved a sigh and added, "Of course, it's also impossible. We couldn't get inside prisons much less take men out."

"'With God, all things are possible,'" I quoted back at him one of his favorite Scripture passages.

"But where would we begin? There are hundreds of prisons; wardens are a hard-nosed bunch." Harold then recounted how as governor of Iowa he had tried to bring about prison reform and had run into every possible obstacle. We spent the morning praying and discussing strategy. Having been in politics so many years, we both thought we knew how to press buttons and make things happen. But this was an awesome challenge.

It was Harold's suggestion that we visit James Eastland, a respected senior member of the U.S. Senate and chairman of the Judiciary Committee, which handles all laws relating to prisons and criminal justice. One call from the chairman and attorneys general have been known to

CHUCK AND GORDON
LOUX, PFM'S SECOND
PRESIDENT, VISITING
INMATES.

stand at attention. His power was legendary in Washington and he used it, quietly but effectively. His support would be crucial.

Despite their political differences—Harold, younger, liberal, and a maverick; Eastland, an older Dixiecrat and conservative—the two men had a warm personal friendship. Two weeks later we were in Eastland's spacious Senate office.

Always the courtly, southern gentleman, Senator Eastland listened patiently as I detailed the horrors of prison life. At one point, he leaned forward, peered through his silver-rimmed glasses, and smiled: "You didn't mind it at Maxwell, did you? That's a nice place." His drawl was so gentle, his round face so kind, I restrained a sharp reply.

"Have you ever been there, Senator?"

"No. Maybe I should. Got a lot of my constituents there," he chuckled.

"Have you ever visited *any* prison, Senator?" I asked.

"No. . . ." He looked reflective, rubbing his chin. "No, I haven't. Pretty busy in this job, you know."

Over and over in the months ahead I was to discover the same pleasant indifference in men who had the fate of thousands of prisoners in their hands. They pass the laws, provide the money, express appropriate horror about the rising crime rate, but beyond that, they just don't care. But then, I reminded myself, I had possessed this kind of power once, and I hadn't cared either.

Senator Eastland listened politely for almost two hours, then suggested we meet with his staff. "You talk to my boys here; then we'll certainly look into doing something like you fellas are talking about.

AS TIME WENT BY, MY CONVICTION DEEPENED THAT GOD HAD GIVEN ME A VISION FOR THE PRISONS.

Mighty interesting and mighty nice seeing you. Keep up the good work, Harold." He slapped his colleague on the back.

That was it. The weeks passed. We heard nothing from Senator Eastland or his staff. We called several times. His staff was always polite; the matter, we were told, was being considered.

I talked with other old friends in Congress. Most of them thought it was a "nice idea" to do something for men in prison. We didn't hear anything further from them either.

As time went by, my conviction deepened that God had indeed given me a vision for a new work in the prisons even though nothing had happened and the doors seemed closed. During one of our regular Monday morning fellowship breakfasts, Harold shook his head: "I don't think we'll get any help from Congress. Politicians are wary of prison work. They know that 80 percent of the public wants to hang criminals. Why should they do anything?"

"What if we went right to the head of the Bureau of Prisons?" I asked, realizing as I said it that it was a foolish idea. Government bureaucrats wouldn't risk giving prisoners furloughs unless there was political heat on them to do so.

"Nothing to lose," Harold mused. "Who is the director?"

"Norman Carlson. He's a career man, nonpolitical, tough, respected. That's all I know." We all agreed with Harold. What could we lose?

Harold beckoned for Doug's secretary, Jo Adamson, to come into the library where we were meeting. "Please call Norman Carlson at the Bureau of Prisons and ask for an appointment for Mr. Colson and me," he instructed her.

Jo is a perceptive young woman. "His

secretary will want to know what it is about," she warned.

Harold looked at us, then shrugged. "Tell her it's about bringing Jesus Christ into prisons," he roared. Jo laughed nervously, then realizing that Harold was serious, nodded and quickly departed.

Jo repeated the message verbatim to a secretary in Norman Carlson's office. We got the appointment for the next day.

On a sunny June morning, Fred Rhodes drove us to the Bureau of Prisons, located just a few blocks from the Capitol. Fred stopped the car outside the entrance, and we prayed together that God would touch Norman Carlson's heart. Fred prayed with such emotion that I hardly heard the horns blowing behind us.

Seven months in prison had created in my mind a stereotype of wardens and prison officials: unfeeling, tight-lipped, hard-nosed bureaucrats. At first glance, Norman Carlson fitted that description. He is a tall, muscular man with a strong, stern face and close-cropped blond hair.

We saw him from his outer reception area, standing in the doorway of his office in shirt sleeves. Suddenly his face relaxed with a friendly grin. "Hi, fellas. Come on in." Then he led us to his large, attractively furnished office.

To our surprise we learned that Carlson had grown up in Iowa, Harold's

home state. He knew and approved of the work Harold had begun in the state prisons while governor.

I studied Carlson as the two began swapping tales about Iowa prisons: He looked efficient, open, a man who'd risen fast through the system. In 1972 he had received a coveted award as one of the ten outstanding persons in government ser-

> **"MR. CARLSON, WE CAME HERE TODAY TO TELL YOU OF A DREAM WE HAVE. . . . WE NEED YOUR COOPERATION."**

vice. But he still was no risk taker, I figured. Government officials have to go to Congress once a year and justify adding millions to their budgets by telling what a good job they and their agencies do. No matter how I phrased it, I was going to be critical of Carlson's prison system, and he could well take it personally.

Harold asked Carlson if he objected to beginning the meeting with prayer. Carlson indicated he did not, and Harold

led us. Then he set the stage. "Mr. Carlson, we came here today to tell you of a dream we have for a new work in the federal prisons. We need your cooperation. Chuck will explain."

I developed the case slowly, depicting my own experiences inside the prisons, what happened with our little fellowship at the Maxwell facility, and how Jesus Christ can touch and change the lives of men in prison. Then I covered point by point what I felt was wrong in the system.

"More than half of those who come out of prison commit new crimes. The repeat-offender rate is 80 percent in some states. Prisons simply do not rehabilitate, Mr. Carlson," I said at one point, pausing to give him a chance to reply. He nodded but didn't say a word.

"We're spending billions on prisons, but four out of five crimes are committed by ex-convicts, according to one study. It's futile and a horrid waste. We must do better, do things to turn lives around. It's the only answer," I said, pausing again. Still no response.

This man's career was to run the prison system, and I was describing it as futile and wasteful. But if he was angry, he didn't show it. He remained silent, his expression inscrutable.

I glanced at Harold; his head was down. I hoped he was praying.

As I continued, Carlson remained attentive. But at any moment I was ready for him to raise his hand and stop me cold. In the system for twenty years, he could easily dismiss my advice and show me the door.

Then I drew a deep breath, wondered momentarily about Carlson's faith, and moved headlong into my final point. "Mr. Carlson, the prisons—your prisons—aren't helping these men. Everybody there, even the best of your staff, are looked upon as cops. But one Person can make a difference: Jesus Christ. His love and power to remake lives is the answer. He will heal and reconcile. I know it. I saw it happen. Give us a chance to prove it."

Still not a muscle moved in Carlson's face.

I asked Norman Carlson if he would issue an order allowing Harold and me, or our representatives, to go into any federal prison in the country and select prisoners to bring out for training. In the moment of silence that followed, I nearly laughed. It sounded preposterous.

"Is that it?" he asked brusquely.

"Yes, sir."

"Well, there's much truth in what you say, gentlemen. I know prisons are not good places—not even the best of them." He paused, and I waited for the "but,"

to be followed by six reasons it could never be done.

Carlson's face remained enigmatic. "Let me ask you a question. A few weeks ago my wife and I were at the Terminal Island Prison in southern California. On Sunday we went to chapel. At one point the chaplain asked the inmates to join in with spontaneous prayers. In the

> I STILL HAD MUCH TO LEARN ABOUT THE WAY GOD WORKS IN OUR LIVES—AND WHAT HE WANTED FROM MINE.

back—I couldn't see him—a man prayed for my wife and me. I was surprised that he did that."

"Well, Mr. Carlson, he's a Christian," I said, after a pause. "We're taught to pray for those in authority. I did for the warden at Maxwell."

"I know that," Carlson replied, his eyes bright with emotion. He raised both hands and pointed all his fingers into his breastbone. "But I'm the one keeping him in prison."

It was an electric moment. "Mr. Carlson," I said, "that man prayed for you because he loves you." Carlson stared deep into my eyes, then shook his head in bewilderment, and the conversation moved back to the prison program.

I expected Carlson to evade my request, knowing from long experience that no government bureau chief would take such a bold step without consulting his staff, weighing the pros and cons, and at least thinking about the impact of his decision on his career. The best I could hope for was that he'd leave the door open just a crack.

I was stunned when, moments later, Carlson gave us a terse, three-sentence answer. "Go ahead with your plans, Mr. Colson, Senator Hughes. I'll issue the order. Get together with my staff and work out the details."

I did not then fully understand all that had happened in Norman Carlson's office that June day. And it would be months before I'd even think again of the unknown inmate in the back of the prison chapel who had prayed for Carlson and his wife. I still had much to learn about the way God works in our lives—and what He wanted from mine.

CHARLES W. COLSON
Adapted from Life Sentence *by Charles Colson, © 1979, published by Chosen Books, Fleming H. Revell Company. Used by permission.*

The huge Dutch-colonial prison in Indonesia was a warehouse for misery. I could see that—despite the flowers lining the walkway leading to the prison chapel. We were already late, but as we hurried past the cell blocks, I peered into their seemingly endless corridors of grimy gray and steel. I could almost taste the foul, stale air of human degradation and despair.

We passed through a small walled courtyard and entered the chapel, packed to capacity. More than the usual number of inmates had turned out to meet the foreign guests.

Some two hundred prisoners sat shoulder to shoulder on close rows of backless benches. Apart from the wheezing fan near the altar, there was no relief from the steamy air of the tropical rainy season.

The long, hot service tested the endurance of my cold Canadian blood, so when the leader of the meeting asked me to simply bring official greetings from Prison Fellowship International, I was only too eager to comply. I delivered greetings from brothers and sisters in prison around the world—in Africa, North America, Latin America, Europe, and Asia.

But as I spoke, I sensed the cosmic futility of those greetings. The eyes before me reflected interest, but in the depths of their expressions I saw a deeper need—something that would never be touched by greetings and tokens of human solidarity alone.

Had I traveled more than nine thousand miles just to come there as an international courier of good will and pleasant words? I had to say more. "But I haven't come here just to bring you news from your brothers and sisters around the

> ...OUR MINISTRY IS TO BRING PEOPLE FACE-TO-FACE WITH JESUS CHRIST....

world—fellow prisoners; I've come here because of a prisoner who changed my life. I've come here because of Jesus Christ, who is the only One who fully understands your pain and circumstances, the only One who takes His place with us in the midst of life's deepest misery. . . ."

After the meeting, shaking hands with the prisoners, I learned that almost half of them were Muslims. A number were political prisoners under sentence of death, men who had been there twenty years, not knowing which day might be their last.

The next day my hectic schedule continued: back-to-back meetings and another prison visit in another city. Again I was compelled to share with the dozen or so inmates the message of their fellow prisoner, Jesus Christ.

Later that evening we received bad news from the prison we had visited the day before. Four men had been executed that morning—four men who had waited twenty years for the dreaded day of execution. Without warning that day had arrived—one day after my visit with three of those men.

I was stunned by disbelief as I listened to the news. What if I had stood before those men on the brink of their eternity and brought simple greetings from other prisoners in other places? What a waste of time and effort. What a squander of a holy trust.

Second Timothy 4:2-5 charges us to preach the Word, to be urgent in season and out of season, to do the work of an evangelist, and to fulfill our ministry.

There should be only one reason why you or I do what we do. Everything we do is ministry, and our ministry is to bring people face-to-face with Jesus Christ—in every season and even out of season.

RONALD W. NIKKEL
From the April 1990 issue of JUBILEE

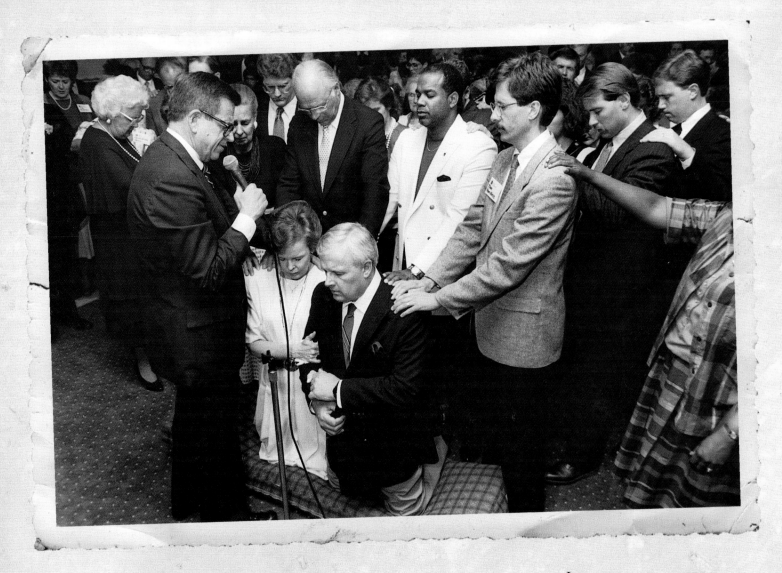

INDUCTION CEREMONY FOR

TOM AND GLORIA PRATT. TOM HAS BEEN PFM'S PRESIDENT SINCE 1989.

CHUCK RECEIVED
THE TEMPLETON
PRIZE FOR PROGRESS
IN RELIGION IN 1993.

FORMER PRESIDENT
JIMMY CARTER AND
CHUCK COLSON
WORK ON A HABITAT
FOR HUMANITY
PROJECT TOGETHER.

WE HAVE A GRAND, GOD-GIVEN OPPOR-
TUNITY—SO THAT THE WORLD MIGHT SEE
THE GLORIES OF THE KINGDOM THROUGH
OUR FAITHFUL OBEDIENCE. IT IS SOCI-
ETY'S ONE HOPE. IT IS THE CHURCH'S
GOD-GIVEN COMMISSION. LET US BE
STEADFAST, ABOUNDING IN GOD'S GRACE
AND DOING OUR DUTY AS HE HAS
CALLED.

—*Chuck Colson*

NOBODY IN EARTHLY PLANNING WOULD
EVER, EVER HAVE STARTED A MINISTRY AT
THE TIME THIS MINISTRY WAS STARTED,
AND CERTAINLY IT WOULD NOT HAVE
BEEN STARTED WITH SUCH AN UNLIKELY
PERSON AS CHUCK COLSON.

—*Fred Rhodes, former president of PFM*

As founder and chairman of the board, Chuck Colson is actively involved in the work of PFM. He visits prisons regularly—including every Easter—and works with the top-level leadership to help guide Prison Fellowship's mission and priorities.

Chuck's unique combination of political and ministry experience has opened up significant opportunities to address a variety of issues that impact the church and society as a whole. Thus, he spends much of his time writing and speaking—challenging the church to a radical lifestyle of obedience to Christ and confronting contemporary values from a biblically informed perspective.

In 1993 Chuck was awarded the Templeton Prize for Progress in Religion, a prestigious, internationally recognized honor that both acknowledged and expanded his influence as a Christian leader and spokesperson. Since all speaking honoraria and royalties from Chuck's writings are given to Prison Fellowship, Chuck also declined the $1 million Templeton Prize, which was given directly to PFM as an endowment for future ministry expansion.

CHUCK AND AL QUIE TALK
WITH AN INMATE. AL QUIE,
IN ADDITION TO BEING THE
FOURTH PRESIDENT OF PFM,
HAS HAD A SIGNIFICANT
IMPACT ON COLSON'S LIFE.

The Last Supper. Jesus knew the time was near: Soon those He had come to save would crucify Him, and those closest to Him would scatter. At this final Passover meal, Jesus admonished His disciples to imitate His love. The Greek word for this love is *agape*—to give oneself for another, to love even one's enemy.

"A new command I give you: Love one another. As I have loved you, so you must love one another," Jesus said emphatically (John 13:34). "But I tell you: Love your enemies and pray for those who persecute you" (Matt. 5:44).

Indeed, those of us who claim faith in Christ must keep Him central and demonstrate love (agape) in all that we do. Certainly such a perspective is crucial for the thousands who reach out to those touched by crime: to prisoners, ex-prisoners, their family members, and victims.

Prison Fellowship has several programs to help men and women involved in prison ministry. But who ministers to our volunteers? Of course, a quick response is that Jesus does, and that is true. But, in addition, other Christians do—those who model agape. That's why we underscore the need for church involvement, for it's in a local church that such loving relationships are nurtured.

The love of fellow Christians also helps ex-inmates to stay out of prison.

The statistics are grim: 74 percent of those incarcerated here in America will be rearrested within four years after release. Even those who claimed victory in Christ while in prison find life outside a constant struggle. But as God works through Christians who live out their faith, demonstrating agape by walking with ex-prisoners and sharing

FOR WHEN A LOST SHEEP IS FOUND, WE REJOICE, AND THIS JOY SPURS US ONWARD.

Christ, these former inmates are strengthened and victorious.

The PFM purpose statement confirms that we seek to assist Christ's church in prison ministry as the Holy Spirit directs. We assist the church in four areas. The first is physical: We make materials available. The second is intellectual: We offer our strategies and messages. The third is moral: We bolster the church morally, encouraging believers to maintain integrity, respect

for others, and compassion. The fourth is spiritual: We strive to offer spiritual nourishment and example through our relationship to God, holy living, and care for the less fortunate. These areas are all important, but each is more important than the former, finally proven in our ability to love.

Christian organizations like PFM must never vie for power or prestige or let pride in one's efforts slip into our ranks. Rather, God must always be our focus, and He will share His glory with no one. As we submit totally to Him, we realize great joy in service. For when a lost sheep is found, we rejoice, and this joy spurs us onward.

As we serve Christ together, it is essential that we live the new life He has given us, practicing His love in all that we do from morning to night, in all of our relationships.

Let me encourage you to keep Christ central, keep His love flowing. Demonstrate His love by building up each other and sharing one another's hardships. I urge you as well to cultivate one-to-one relationships.

"This is my command: Love each other" (John 15:17).

ALBERT H. QUIE
From the July 1988 issue of JUBILEE

Not one to shy away from controversial topics, PFM Chairman Chuck Colson speaks out in a four-minute weekday radio program, offering his perspective on current events. Aired on 325 stations nationwide, *BreakPoint* is also available on-line through CompuServe on the Christian Interactive Network.

PATTY COLSON:
I Will Stand with You

I HAD BEEN WRESTLING FOR OVER A YEAR ABOUT WHETHER I SHOULD GO INTO THE MINISTRY OR NOT. THEN ONE NIGHT, AS WE WERE SITTING AND LOOKING AT THE SUN SETTING OVER THE OCEAN, PATTY JUST LEANED OVER AND SAID, "I KNOW WHAT YOU'RE ANGUISHING OVER, AND IF YOU BELIEVE IT'S GOD'S CALL TO GO INTO THE PRISONS, THEN I WILL STAND WITH YOU." BECAUSE OF THAT, THE MINISTRY STARTED TWENTY YEARS AGO—PATTY'S WORDS FREED ME TO DO IT.

—*Chuck Colson*

WITHOUT PATTY THERE WOULD BE NO CHUCK COLSON, JUST PUT IT THAT WAY. MOST PEOPLE CONSIDER PATTY ONLY AS THE WIFE OF CHUCK COLSON, BUT THAT'S TOO SIMPLE. THEY'RE A TEAM, AND IF IT WASN'T FOR HER AND HER VISION, HER HEART AND HER COMMITMENT, HER STICKING BY, I WOULD SAY THERE WOULDN'T BE ANY PRISON FELLOWSHIP. SHE'S A TREMENDOUS PERSON.

—*Doug Coe*

INSIDE JOURNAL IS SENT TO EVERY FEDERAL PRISON IN THE U.S., REACHING AN ESTIMATED TOTAL OF FIVE HUNDRED THOUSAND INMATES.

ENTRIES IN THE TRIENNIAL PRISONERS' ART CONTEST.

THE PRISON
FELLOWSHIP NATIONAL
OFFICE IS LOCATED IN
NORTHERN VIRGINIA.

IV | GUIDING THE LOST

PRISONS WERE ONCE CLOSED TO CHRISTIAN WITNESS, BUT GOD HAS OPENED

DOORS OF OPPORTUNITY. PRISON ADMINISTRATORS—WITNESSING THE

DIFFERENCE CHRIST MAKES IN A PRISONER'S LIFE—ARE ASKING PFM FOR

MORE CHRISTIAN PROGRAMMING. STUDYING THE BIBLE CHANGES LIVES.

High above the prison auditorium's hardwood floors, fluorescent lights hum to life, turning back the early autumn dusk that has settled across the plains of eastern Oregon.

In the silence of the empty auditorium, Prison Fellowship volunteer leader Steve Kirkeby readies the overhead projector. Music leader—and Steve's pastor—Bill Miller tunes his guitar.

Suddenly, tromping feet thunder on the outside fire escape. A long string of prisoners has begun its three-story ascent from the courtyard of Eastern Oregon Correctional Institution.

The men burst into the light noisily, chattering and smiling. Backslaps and handshakes greet Steve, Bill, and the other PFM volunteers, including Steve's wife, Verla.

For five minutes, "How you doin', brother?" "Praise the Lord!" and "Amen, praise Him!" fill the air as eighty-nine prisoners clad in denim mill about the auditorium—old and young men, white and black, Hispanic, Asian. Men with shaved heads. Men with dreadlocks. Together in assembly.

The noise dies down as Steve motions the men to their seats. He speaks into a microphone: "I'm glad to see everybody here tonight."

"Praise the Lord!" erupts from the sea of prisoners before him. Bill and his guitar bring the crowd to its feet, clapping and singing. "O Lord our Lord, how majestic is your name in all the earth!" The inmates clap and wave their arms in praise—song after song after song. Some fifteen to twenty minutes later, they wind down with "Behold the Lamb on His Throne."

> "PRAISE THE LORD!" AND "AMEN, PRAISE HIM!" FILL THE AIR AS EIGHTY-NINE PRISONERS MILL ABOUT THE AUDITORIUM.

The men in the front row count off, "One! Two! Three! . . . " Under the watchful eyes of the correctional officers, prisoners shuffle their chairs into seven circles. Fifteen Spanish speakers form one group. Each small group is led by a PFM volunteer or a prisoner trained for the role.

Tonight's Scripture is Matthew 10:26-33. The key verse: "Whoever acknowledges me before men, I will also acknowledge him before my Father in heaven" (v. 32). As the men analyze the passage, they aren't distracted by the noise and echo in the large room; they simply huddle closer together, intent on hearing what other group members have to say.

Like any Bible study, each group has its talkers and its listeners. Participation is encouraged, and no comment, no insight goes without some rejoinder.

When Steve calls "time," each group in turn sends a spokesman to the microphone to share insights with the larger group. "Is there a promise we can claim?" Steve asks as the last speaker to return to his chair.

Voices call back, "Yes!"

"He will acknowledge us if we acknowledge Him."

"Amen!"

"God knows every hair on our head. He will provide!"

"Praise the Lord!"

As the evening ends, the men rise for prayer. One brother will be paroled next week. "We love him, Lord. We know You want him to succeed," Steve prays. "We pray that his life would give You praise."

The church behind bars sways quietly to "Amazing Grace," then raises the roof on an added last verse: "Praise God. . . ."

The evening closes as it began—
smiles, laughter, handshakes, backslaps.

"Take care, Bill."

"God bless you, Steve. See you next
week!"

Some linger in the light before
prison regimen pulls them down the fire
escape, across the courtyard, and back to
their cells, where many of them will
acknowledge their Lord before their fellow prisoners.

Their voices fade away as a guard locks
the auditorium door behind them. But
the ring of praise lingers as Steve, Verla,
Bill, and the other PFM volunteers gather
their instruments of grace—Bibles, note-
books, overhead sheets, guitar. Steve sits
down to catch his breath, then joins the
others as they head out the front door.
Steve pauses at the entrance and looks
back into the auditorium.

He smiles and turns off the lights.

DAVID CARLSON
From the November 1993 issue of JUBILEE

In 1995 there were 1,237

ongoing Bible studies for

prisoners.

In-Prison Seminars were created to address the needs of prisoners in a way that will help them take responsibility for their lives and experience positive change.

Seminars include the Life Plan Seminar, preparing prisoners near release for life outside the prison; Marriage Seminars, which teach prisoners and their spouses how to strengthen their relationship and communication; Discipleship Seminars, where prisoners learn the basics of the Christian faith; and Financial Seminars, designed to help the prisoner learn how to deal with money matters inside and outside of prison.

All seminars are taught by certified volunteer instructors, who work closely with a team of volunteer small-group leaders responsible for guiding discussions and other activities. Seminars focus on issues of self-worth, relationships, authority, temptation, sex, and others. In 1995, 2,114 seminars were held. In-Prison Seminars are generally followed up with Bible studies and/or mentoring relationships, where volunteers "come alongside" prisoners to consistently offer friendship, counsel, accountability, and a positive role model.

A Prison Fellowship Marriage Seminar helped Elvin and Evelyn Martes rebuild close family relationships.

Elvin Martes (above, right) wasn't used to hugs when he met then-PFM Area Director Gordon Barnes. But Gordon soon got him into the habit.

Pulling her infant and two toddlers close, Evelyn Martes flinched and crossed the crowded jail waiting room. Four-year-old Vinnie clutched his mother's pants leg. "You're a good-looking woman," her husband, Elvin, had told her. Now other men's leering eyes confirmed the appraisal.

"It was the most disgusting place," Evelyn recalls of the Philadelphia detention center, where Elvin was held in 1986. "Every time I took the kids there, they'd get sick. Emotionally, it was tough. So I just went away."

Far away—to live with relatives in Puerto Rico. Foreseeing a long prison term for drug charges, Elvin encouraged Evelyn to leave him—permanently: "Forget about me."

Although she was angry and frustrated over the incarceration, Evelyn's love for Elvin never diminished. "In spite of what he did, he wasn't a tough, mean person."

Youthful greed, not meanness, had launched Elvin's drug-dominated lifestyle. He'd spurned school in the fifth grade, enticed by the income of a factory job finagled with a forged birth certificate.

He started dabbling with marijuana—first for the thrill, then for the money from dealing.

As a teen Elvin faced a new opportunity: "Here, man, see if you can sell it," a fellow drug dealer had urged. "It" was cocaine. And coke meant big money.

Elvin threw his money into cars, motorcycles, a video store, a sporting goods store. "I had plenty of possessions, plenty of free time—what everybody dreams about. Once you have everything, you're supposed to be happy, aren't you?"

But happiness eluded Elvin. "I was always drinking or drugged up." Married

> ## "ONCE YOU HAVE EVERYTHING, YOU'RE SUPPOSED TO BE HAPPY, AREN'T YOU?"

at seventeen, he hid his lifestyle from Evelyn, a gentle, strictly reared Catholic who cared for their three children and turned a deaf ear to friends' warnings.

But illusions crumbled in early 1986 when police swept through the door of Elvin's video store. At age twenty-two, the man who had "everything" lost it all for eight kilos of seized coke.

But that loss led Elvin to find what he really needed. Sentenced to Allenwood Federal Correctional Institution, Elvin skeptically accepted an inmate's invitation to a Bible study. "I expected a holy roller ready to cram the Bible down our throats," he remembers. Instead, he was wrapped in a warm bear hug. The gesture shocked and soothed him: "I wasn't used to that, you know!"

The soothing "bear" was Prison Fellowship volunteer Gordon Barnes—now PFM area director in Williamsport, Pennsylvania. Elvin didn't know Gordon's past: As a younger man Gordon would have sooner hugged a rifle—cocked to blow a prisoner's head off—than a prisoner. During a jail escape an inmate wielding a pipe had brutally beaten Gordon's deputy-warden father. "When someone hurts your father—I would have shot him," Gordon admits.

From a hospital bed, Gordon's father "looked me right in the eye and knew I was consumed with hate," Gordon remembers. "He said, 'I forgive them; you've got to forgive them.' And it did something to me."

Released from his hate, Gordon went on to become a correctional officer, a job he left in 1973. Five years later he began volunteering for prison ministry. He explains, "I saw how forsaken and forgotten these guys were by their families, by their friends."

So Gordon went to them, sharing the reality of the Christian life—sometimes

To prepare for prison ministry,

PFM has a twenty-hour training session for its volunteers.

LeRoy Buck—now a PFM employee—was in prison.

This volunteer is reading to an inmate. Between 50 and 75 percent of prisoners are functionally illiterate.

DAVID SPOUNG,
A COMMITTED
VOLUNTEER FOR
YEARS, FAITHFULLY
VISITS AND MENTORS
THE IMPRISONED.

even the downside.

"It's important that the inmates know that God uses ordinary people," Gordon says of himself and his wife and prison-ministry partner, Diann. "I've shared my adversities. We've always tried to be real, right up front."

"That's one of the things I admired," Elvin says of his Bible-teacher-turned-mentor. "You run into holy rollers who paint everything so beautiful. But Gordon was telling us both sides of the story. And that's what made me want to come back for more."

"More" was a steady diet of Bible studies, prayer meetings, and PFM seminars, which helped solidify Elvin's commitment to Christ and encouraged him to share it with Evelyn.

In October 1988 Elvin encouraged Evelyn to come to Allenwood for a PFM Marriage Seminar. "I wanted her to see that I had changed," Elvin says.

After a few hesitant questions—"Can I wear pants? makeup?"—Evelyn decided to go, facing her husband for the first time in eighteen months. And PFM staff and volunteers rallied around her, paying hotel expenses for her and the children.

"The efforts were worth it," says Gordon, who saw two people deeply in love. Gordon speaks admiringly of Evelyn: "A lot of women would have already written a 'Dear John' letter. And

for her to stick it out with him for two years spoke volumes."

Learning that Jesus could be her husband while her husband was away, Evelyn committed her life to Christ and began to study the Bible.

While the seminar offered a therapeutic shot in the arm, subsequent mentoring gave hope for steady recovery.

> ELVIN AND EVELYN ARE LIVING PROOF THAT JESUS CHANGES LIVES.

Gordon and Diann, together with PFM volunteers Walt and Vickie Persing, took the Marteses under their wing, counseling and encouraging them. Those bonds proved strong when Elvin was released on parole in July 1989.

But freedom came with a new set of difficulties and an old set of temptations. Although Elvin quickly found a job with a Philadelphia construction company, the income topped out far below his preprison days. "I know guys

that came out [of prison] the same time that I did. You know what they're driving now? BMWs and Corvettes. Their houses look like palaces."

By contrast, the five Marteses moved into one cramped room of a relative's basement. "We didn't have anything, and I was getting disgusted," Elvin confesses. "I even started drinking a little. I'd say, 'Evelyn, we've got to do something quick, because I'm getting to the point—'"

"And I would tell him, 'Sit down, wake up, and smell the coffee!'" Evelyn cuts in. "'I was out here alone with three kids. I survived. You can, too.'"

"Yeah, she helped me a lot through that rough period until we got our own house," Elvin says. "She stuck it out with me, so I could stick it out for her and the kids."

Two hours away, in Williamsport, Gordon was also "on call" with a supportive word. Hardships plus rekindled temptations—"Those are the kinds of things that cause men to go back to prison," Gordon says. "Thank God I was there for Elvin to call."

Elvin has also faced adjustments as an at-home dad to Vinnie (eight), Tony (five), and Whitney (four), although Evelyn tried to make this transition as smooth as possible. "Every night we'd look at pictures of 'Poppy' and give him a kiss," she explains. "And when he called from prison, he always spoke to them.

But after he came home, they were shy. They weren't used to having him there."

But Dad and kids have found common interests. They canvass the back woods and creek, hunting for salamanders, turtles, and snakes. And when second-grader Vinnie pulls out his homework, Elvin cracks the books too. Dad is now back in school two nights a week, pursuing a high school equivalency diploma.

In his "spare" time Elvin, along with other members of Northeast Assembly of God, are organizing a support group for ex-prisoners, hoping to draw men from the local halfway house.

"They sense a security when they see Elvin has made it," Evelyn says of her husband's recent visit to the halfway house. "But if another guy got to them first—someone who was successful doing the same [illegal] thing again—they might go back, too."

"That's why this is so important to me," says Elvin, who is working with a local car-parts manufacturer to provide jobs for ex-prisoners.

Gordon, eager to help Elvin in his ministry endeavors, encourages the Marteses to share their testimony in churches. "I consider them a miracle," Gordon affirms. "Elvin and Evelyn are living proof that Jesus changes lives."

BECKY BEANE
from the July 1991 issue of JUBILEE

I can still remember the day: June 6, 1984. I was sitting in a courtroom. I stood and watched as my husband was handcuffed and was taken to prison.

I was totally devastated. I couldn't believe that after being married and having a family together, this would happen to us. He walked through that door, and I was completely alone.

I hated him. He left me with problems, kids, bills. He didn't have to do anything but serve time.

I hated this man. I knew if he was in prison I could divorce him because he couldn't do anything to stop it.

The children were small and didn't understand that their dad was in prison. I went a couple times to see him, but I didn't like what I saw. He was happy—he took everything so lightly. It irritated me. I thought, *What is going on? Why are you so happy?* Nothing made sense.

After four or five weeks of visits, he told me that the prison was going to have a special thing for couples, where wives can come in and spend a day with their husband. "At least we'll be able to be together," he said. He didn't know I wanted to divorce him.

I thought, *I'm going to do this one last thing for this man.* I went to this gathering. Well, my husband neglected to tell me it was a **Prison Fellowship Marriage Seminar!**

Well, guess what happened? I accepted the Lord! But on the drive home, I yelled at the Lord. *They just told me the Bible says I can't divorce. I'm stuck!*

In our state there was a marriage seminar each month, and we participated in every one of them. The seminars taught us how to communicate while we were apart. There was a lot of counseling, facing one another, and dealing with situations we never would have dreamed of having to talk to each other about.

After my husband came home, we had counseling and people helping us. Today, this man is loved more than he has ever been loved before. I owe this to the Lord, for if it were not for Prison Fellowship Ministries, we would have divorced. Yes, we've had many tragedies, but the Lord is with us.

In the words of one spouse

V | THE GIFT OF HOPE

THE PLAN IS SIMPLE; THE REWARDS ARE GREAT. BY BUYING

AND DELIVERING CHRISTMAS GIFTS FOR PRISONERS'

CHILDREN—PRESENTING THE GIFTS AS BEING FROM THE

ABSENT PARENT—ANGEL TREE® VOLUNTEERS BRING LOVE,

JOY, AND GRACE INTO THE HEARTS OF FAMILIES.

"What does 265,000 even look like? It's mind boggling!" exclaimed Mary Kay Beard when she heard the number of children reached through Angel Tree 1992. [In 1995 Angel Tree reached 463,000 children.] Ten years ago as a volunteer area director for Prison Fellowship Alabama, Mary Kay, an ex-prisoner, spearheaded the first Prison Fellowship Angel Tree.

Looking back, Mary Kay says, "I'm so grateful that God allowed me to be there at the beginning."

That "beginning" was first seeded about twenty years ago when Mary Kay, at "rock bottom" in a solitary-confinement cell, gave her life to Christ while reading a Bible. That year Christmas held a new meaning for her—the birth of her Savior.

But Christmas in prison touched another chord in Mary Kay.

Her gifts? Toothpaste and soap brought in by local church groups. "I had enough toothpaste to last until July!" she says, laughing. But many of her fellow prisoners didn't laugh at the practical gifts. They carefully traded and hoarded them, dividing them lovingly among their children on Christmas "family day."

"Can you imagine wrapping up a miniature tube of toothpaste and a bar of soap to give to your child for Christmas?" Mary Kay asks. "Most children wouldn't think much of such small gifts, but in prison there was such joy on their faces! It didn't really matter to them what they got; it was from Mama."

Those Christmas images stuck with Mary Kay after her release in 1976 until five years later when she began working with PFM in Alabama. After

> ## "IT DIDN'T REALLY MATTER TO THEM WHAT THEY GOT; IT WAS FROM MAMA."

speaking on prison ministry at a luncheon, Mary Kay listened patiently as one woman vented the common "lock 'em up and throw away the key" sentiment. But when Mary Kay mentioned the children of prisoners, her opponent suddenly softened: "I haven't even thought about them having kids."

An idea sparked: The woman explained how a mall in her hometown had urged shoppers to buy Christmas gifts for poor children. Could something similar be done for prisoners' kids?

Mary Kay thought so and soon gathered support from other PFM volunteers. The plan was to erect Christmas trees in malls, encouraging shoppers to buy presents for specific children. Then someone suggested writing the children's names on paper ornaments shaped like angels. An "Angel Tree"!

At first, local mall managers balked. But with persistence, PFM received permission from shopping malls in Birmingham and Montgomery. And on the day after Thanksgiving 1982—the busiest retail day of the year—a tree greeted shoppers at the top of the malls' escalators.

To get names for the angels, Mary Kay had called prison chaplains, then visited prisoners to encourage them to sign up for gifts for their children—to be given on the inmates' behalf. "You know, God never wastes anything," she recalls. "He used my own criminal past to give me credibility in their eyes. And they trusted us."

But Mary Kay admits that her vision was limited. "We thought if we could provide gifts for 200, maybe 300 children, we'd be doing well." That first year Angel Tree gave gifts to 556 children.

"Knowing that they were meeting a specific need, the shoppers were generous beyond our wildest imagination," says Mary Kay. "We were bold that first year; we asked for four gifts per child. And every single child got all four gifts!"

Mary Kay knew the children would be delighted by Angel Tree. What she didn't anticipate was its impact on the prisoners—and on PFM's other programs. "Around January and February our PFM Bible studies and seminars increased dramatically. Inmates were asking, 'Is this the same group that got Christmas for my kids? I think I'll go to this seminar.' And, of course, that opened the door to share the love of Christ."

She saw another result, too: a reuniting of family ties, as children who had not heard from Dad for a while now received gifts from him.

Branching to twelve states the following year—and soon restructured as a church-based program—Angel Tree is now PFM's most popular program, winning hearts throughout the U.S. and in more than ten other countries.

Knowing that makes Mary Kay smile. "Being there at the beginning— I consider it one of the highest privileges of my life."

BECKY BEANE
From the March 1993 issue of JUBILEE

MARY KAY BEARD,

THE FOUNDER

OF ANGEL TREE.

"Little did I know that God would use something like Angel Tree—just simple toys and simple presents—to bless my family, to turn my wife around." There's joy in the voice of ex-prisoner José Abreu. And gratitude. And wonder.

"It was a gift from heaven," says José's wife, Mayra. "That's what we thought when we received that [Angel Tree] package four years ago on Christmas Eve." Mayra had been living on the edge, addicted to crack cocaine. After three years of shuffling back and forth between welfare hotels and homeless shelters, she and her three children had precariously settled in a Queens, New York, public-housing apartment.

"I would go to sleep scared," says daughter Mencia, now a pretty, street-wise twelve-year-old, recalling life in the shelters. "All my mother's friends were on drugs, and they could come in anytime . . . not even friends—strangers out of nowhere. We were scared twenty-four hours [a day]."

Mencia remembers hearing gunfire at night. "I was afraid for my mother . . . that she would be dead somewhere."

Even at age seven, Mencia knew the drugs were destroying her family. "Why are you doing this, Mom? What's the matter with you?"

Mayra always had an empty answer for her daughter's pleas: "Mencia, Mencia, I'm going to stop, I promise."

The drugs had already stolen away Mencia's dad, arrested in April 1988 for two of countless burglaries committed to feed his hungry addiction.

Mencia tearfully recalls José's absence. "It's hard not to have a father.

> "WHY ARE YOU DOING THIS, MOM? WHAT IS THE MATTER WITH YOU?"

. . . I believed in him so much. . . . Even when he was in prison . . . I loved him the same."

And even in a psychiatric institution for the criminally insane, wasted José found a Christian volunteer who loved him and believed in him enough to introduce him to Christ, who transformed José's life.

Later, in Franklin Correctional Facility, José attended Prison Fellowship seminars and Bible studies. With the enthusiasm of a new convert, José wanted to share his life-changing faith with his family—especially Mayra.

"Unfortunately, I got real pushy about it," says José, who showered Mayra with leaflets, tracts, and Bibles. He even arranged for prison volunteers to visit Mayra and to witness to her. But Mayra wanted nothing to do with Christ. And, admits José, "the more I pushed, the farther away she got from wanting Christianity."

Then in autumn 1989, without much thought or expectation, José signed up for his children to receive Christmas gifts through Angel Tree to be purchased by PFM volunteers but delivered "from Dad."

"I filled out the applications," José remembers, "thinking it was just routine, like many other things—and many other promises."

When José mentioned Angel Tree to Mayra, she didn't pay much attention either, even though she hadn't bought any gifts for the children. She intended to, of course, if she could just hold on to some money.

Then, on Christmas Eve, just before Mayra and the children left their apartment to spend a meager Christmas at Mayra's sister's, someone knocked at the door.

What makes the Abreu family jump for joy? The memory of an unexpected Christmas gift that helped turn Mom from drugs to Christ.

While behind bars, José Abreu signed up his family for Angel Tree gifts, not knowing that his actions would lead to their salvation. From left: José, sons Alejandro and Enriquillo, mom Mayra, foster baby Isaac, and daughter Mencia.

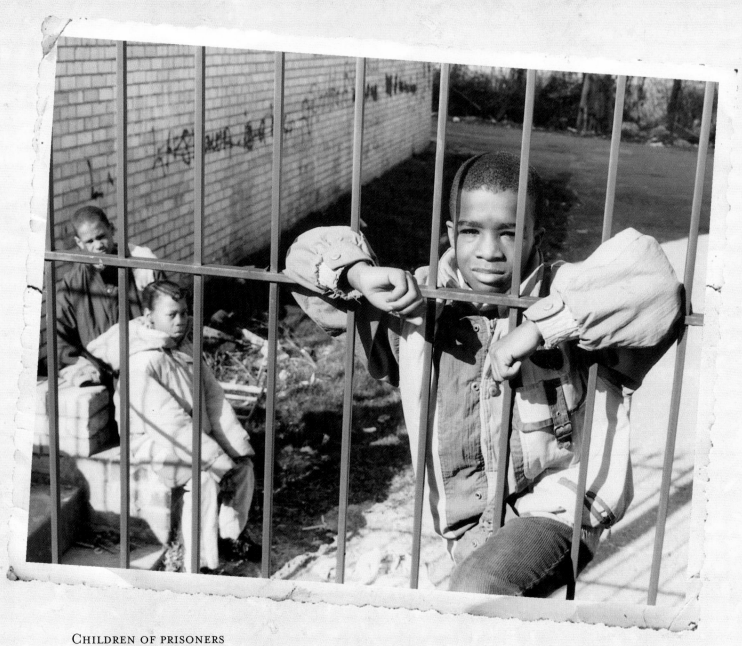

CHILDREN OF PRISONERS

ARE DEPRIVED OF MANY

NORMAL CHILDHOOD

EXPERIENCES.

"There was a UPS guy with a BIG box," says Mayra. "We took the box into the living room and opened it. It said, 'From José Abreu.' José Abreu? How could it be? José's in jail. He can't buy anything! Then it clicked in my mind . . . Angel Tree!"

The kids went crazy. "It's from Daddy!" Mencia shouted. "Dad is thinking of us! Dad got us this!"

Tears welled up in Mayra's eyes as she recalls, "My kids were crying and jumping up and down and hugging me shouting, 'Mommy! Look what I have!'"

A doll for Mencia. A space shuttle and a toy farm for the younger boys, Alejandro and Enriquillo. Clothes for everyone.

"That is when I cried out to God, and I knew that He loved me," says Mayra. "I accepted the Lord Jesus Christ into my life.

"And then I prayed with my kids," Mayra continues. "I said, 'God, please help me to stop this bad habit I have . . . I don't want it anymore. . . . Take this drug addiction away from me, please, so I can be a responsible parent . . . the mom they deserve to have.'"

At that moment Jesus delivered Mayra from her addiction. The Abreu family was free at last. It was a gift from heaven.

"When Mom accepted Christ, I was right there," says Mencia, "and I accepted Christ with her.

"It's a total change for our family—reuniting, getting to know what life is all about."

And José was part of that reuniting, coming home to his family in July 1990. "I didn't walk out of prison by

> "IT'S A TOTAL CHANGE FOR OUR FAMILY—REUNITING, GETTING TO KNOW WHAT LIFE IS ALL ABOUT."

myself," José proclaims. "I brought Jesus with me."

José now runs a computer shop with his brothers and is pursuing a bachelor's degree in psychology. Mayra works as an accounting secretary. Both serve their Lord in the prison ministry of Coney Island Gospel Assembly. José is also president of the New Cornerstone Adoption Program, which provides practical assistance to female prisoners

at the Rose M. Singer Center. Josè and Mayra, for instance, are taking care of baby Isaac—born behind bars—until his mother is released.

Last spring José and Mayra agreed to give their testimony at a New York City PFM fund-raising banquet. As they stood behind the podium at the Sheraton Hotel, they gave thanks to God, who delivered them through Angel Tree.

To this day they do not know the identity of the PFM volunteer or volunteers who sent that UPS package on José's behalf. Whoever you are, José and Mayra—and Mencia and her brothers—say thank you. To them, you are "a gift from heaven."

DAVID CARLSON
JOHN SHAW
From the December 1993 issue of JUBILEE

SOME CHURCHES CHOOSE
TO HAVE AN ANGEL TREE
PARTY, WHERE THE
CHILDREN COME TO THE
CHURCH AND CELEBRATE
CHRISTMAS. FOR MANY
FAMILIES WHO WOULD
NOT NORMALLY GO TO
CHURCH FOR HELP, THIS
INITIAL EXPERIENCE
OPENS DOORS TO
RELATIONSHIPS BEYOND
THE GIFT-GIVING.

VOLUNTEERS OFFER
ANGEL TREE
REGISTRATION FORMS
TO ALL INMATES.

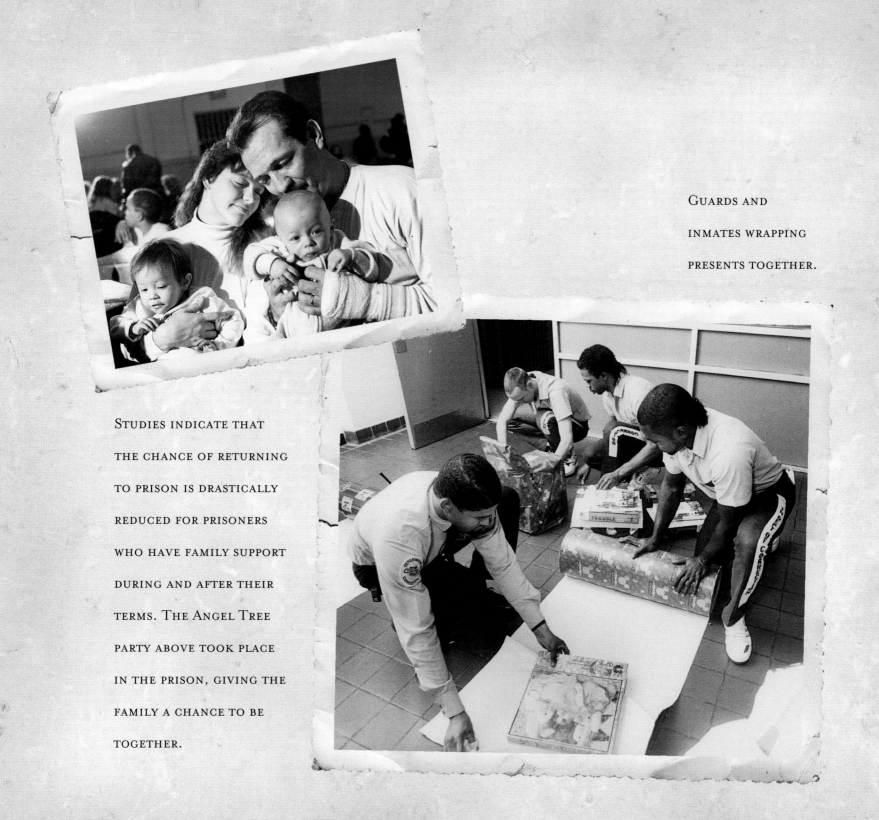

GUARDS AND
INMATES WRAPPING
PRESENTS TOGETHER.

STUDIES INDICATE THAT
THE CHANCE OF RETURNING
TO PRISON IS DRASTICALLY
REDUCED FOR PRISONERS
WHO HAVE FAMILY SUPPORT
DURING AND AFTER THEIR
TERMS. THE ANGEL TREE
PARTY ABOVE TOOK PLACE
IN THE PRISON, GIVING THE
FAMILY A CHANCE TO BE
TOGETHER.

HOOKED ON ANGEL TREE

What Got You Hooked on PFM's Angel Tree Christmas-Gift Project for Prisoners' Children?

My main motivation for getting started with Angel Tree was that I was incarcerated in 1981. In prison I didn't have the funds to buy my ten-year-old son presents. I never felt so useless in all my life; I was used to taking care of him, yet I was unable to do so.

I started Angel Tree in Charlotte by getting churches involved. Regardless of what people feel about inmates, this is for the children. And it's hands-on ministry—not an anonymous gift giveaway.

Besides the people they touch, the volunteers' lives also change once they go out and see the daily experience of prisoners' families. There's also a chance to build a relationship with the inmate, who might come to a PFM Bible study and ask, "Why did these people go out and do this? Boy, it touched my life."

GEORGE FRANKLIN
Angel Tree coordinator for the Charlotte, North Carolina, area since 1985

Once, while I was visiting in the Federal Correctional Institution, La Tuna [Texas], an inmate told me how happy he was that his daughter had received a present from PFM. He asked me to contact the area director to thank him. I wrote the area director, who called me and said they were going to start Angel Tree in El Paso. We started with 127 children's names on a tree. Last Christmas we had 643.

What holds me with it? This is my Christmas! I get so involved and have talked to so many people—the children's guardians and wonderful church people.

An inmate told us last year that Christmas is so lonely; you just sit there and think about home. But he said it made a difference to know that his son would be opening a gift from him. Things like that and the enthusiasm of the volunteers who go to all extremes to get these gifts to the children—that's what holds me.

DORCAS WILKINSON
Angel Tree coordinator for the El Paso, Texas, area since 1984

A group in our church, People-Helper Ministries, got involved with PFM and Angel Tree five years ago to address the needs of prisoners' children. The Bible mandates that we are to put our faith into action, and [Angel Tree] was a significant way to get involved with prisoners.

To have a one-on-one connection with people through Angel Tree—I think that makes all the difference in the world. We have no problem getting people to volunteer to do this because people are eager for their children to learn to give and to be exposed [to another environment].

Last year virtually every prisoner's family we served—150 children—was from one section of Pittsburgh. That was striking because we live in a Norman Rockwell–type of community. It's important for us as a congregation—many of whom are rather affluent—to be giving of ourselves and to be stretched.

MARTHA DANIEL
Angel Tree co-coordinator with husband, Dave, for St. Stephen's Episcopal Church, Sewickley, Pennsylvania, since 1988

My children came to see me today, and it really made me feel good when my little girl said, "Daddy, this sweater you got me is so pretty."

—*inmate*

Making an Angel

Tree delivery.

I CAN'T TELL YOU HOW THE CHILDREN'S FACES LIT UP WHEN THEY OPENED [THEIR PRESENTS]. MY GRANDDAUGHTER BARELY TAKES OFF THE BLACK PANTS SO I CAN WASH THEM. AND MY GRANDSON SAID NOW HE FEELS LIKE THE REST OF THE KIDS, NOT A BUM.

—grandmother guardian

THANK YOU VERY MUCH FOR YOUR HELP. YOU MADE MY KIDS VERY HAPPY AND PROUD OF ME LAST CHRISTMAS. PLEASE TELL MY KIDS I LOVE THEM.

—note from prisoner signing up his children

WOULD YOU PLEASE TELL MY DADDY THAT I SAID THANK YOU FOR THE PRESENT AND THAT I'M NOT MAD AT HIM ANYMORE?

—note an Angel Tree child handed to a North Carolina volunteer

My husband made a special point to say, "We are delivering these for your dad. They are from him." The boy looked a little embarrassed and said under his breath, "Wow," and smiled.

—*church volunteer*

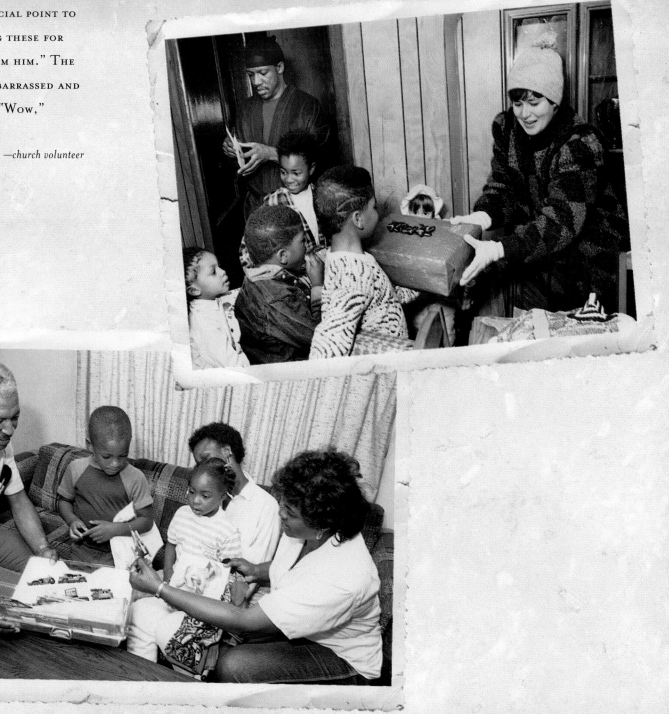

VI | ON THE RIGHT TRACK

WHERE EX-OFFENDERS HAD LITTLE HOPE OF MAKING AN HONEST

GO OF IT ON THE OUTSIDE, PFM MENTORS HAVE RALLIED BEHIND

THESE MEN AND WOMEN, HELPING THEM FIND JOBS, HOUSING, AND

CHRISTIAN FELLOWSHIP TO STAY ON THE STRAIGHT AND NARROW.

Rickey Krogh, an ex-prisoner from Lincoln, Nebraska, recently cringed when he read a line in his local newspaper, the *Journal-Star:* "Once a criminal, I guess, always a criminal."

Rickey knew that this is simply not the case—for himself and for many others released from prison each year.

"That not only upset me but probably upset thousands of other ex-inmates," Rickey wrote in a published letter to the editor. He noted that countless ex-offenders have "discovered that being a productive citizen was worth far more than being a criminal."

Rickey has successfully made the critical transition from inmate to contributing citizen. And he now spends a great deal of time helping others achieve the same goal. He heads up Lincoln's mentoring and support groups for ex-offenders organized by Prison Fellowship's area directors and local churches.

The program takes its name from one of Paul's epistles. From his prison cell in Rome, the apostle wrote to Philemon. The letter is an appeal for Philemon to accept Onesimus, a slave who had apparently robbed Philemon, his well-to-do master, and then run away. In Rome Onesimus had become a Christian as a result of Paul's ministry.

It seems Paul advised Onesimus to return to Philemon. But he didn't send him back empty-handed; he provided a letter of support, in which he encouraged Philemon to welcome Onesimus as a brother in Christ—not as a criminal. "Formerly he was useless to you," Paul writes, "but now he has become useful both to you and to me" (Philemon 1:11). Paul was able to see Onesimus's great potential. Interestingly, tradition says that

> COUNTLESS EX-OFFENDERS DISCOVER BEING A PRODUCTIVE CITIZEN IS WORTH FAR MORE THAN BEING A CRIMINAL.

Onesimus eventually became the bishop of Berea.

We here at Prison Fellowship also believe that ex-offenders have something of value to contribute to society. The mentoring program, through its individual chapters, is reaching out to people like Onesimus—men and women who have experienced the life-changing power of Jesus Christ. Each group, made up entirely of ex-prisoners, is closely tied to a local church. In fact, most Philemon Fellowship meetings are held in churches, which receive former prisoners, not as "ex-convicts," but as fellow believers.

At regular meetings, participants help one another work through the special problems, both physical and spiritual, that ex-inmates must face. They also read and study the Bible and pray for one another. Relationships are made, and members become accountable. Together they find strength in the midst of the struggle to make it on the outside.

"Every one of the members would testify that going back to criminal ways is not an alternative," Rickey wrote in his letter to the *Star.* "They have devoted their lives to becoming productive citizens of our community and are helping other ex-inmates do the same." Indeed, the chain of crime is broken each time an ex-offender makes this successful transition.

Last year, we worked with local church leaders to start six of these groups. Today, there are twenty-four, and thirty-four more are in the planning stages. They are a part of Prison Fellowship's total outreach, which takes inmates from their initial dedication of faith in Christ to their involvement as contributing members in a local church and community after their release.

GORDON D. LOUX
From the May 1987 issue of JUBILEE

Meeting with other
ex-prisoners to talk
about how to make
a successful
transition into life
outside prison.

When in prison, Ray was a solid lay leader.

"For three years I read nothing but the Bible—no other books or newspapers or magazines. I had time to get to know God and to memorize His Word. I didn't spend all my time reading. I helped organize PFM Bible studies. I led a Spanish worship service."

When Ray got out of prison, he hooked in to a church. When he needed a job, a deacon employed him to load trucks. Ray did stay firmly grounded in his faith. He's been out of prison for seven years and has been a PFM staff member. But Ray reflects and offers a sobering dose of reality:

"Sometimes, for a quick second, I've been under such pressure out here that I've thought that it was easier in there—in prison. I shake myself awake real fast. If I—who have a solid family, church support, and years of Bible study under my belt—feel that way sometimes, how must a guy feel if he's leaving prison with no job skills, no support system, no reason to hope?"

I WAS SCARED TO LEAVE PRISON AFTER ELEVEN YEARS, BUT I FELT THAT I COULD MAKE IT "OUT THERE"—WITH SOME HELP. THEN NIELS BEGAN TO VISIT ME [IN PRISON]. NIELS IS MY MENTOR, MY POWERFUL EXAMPLE. HE HELPED SHOW ME THE WAY TO JESUS CHRIST. BUT HE ALSO INSTRUCTED ME IN PRACTICAL THINGS.

—ex-prisoner Jay

I HELPED JAY FIND THE JOB HE NEEDED TO MAKE PAROLE AND GOT HIM A PLACE TO LIVE. GUYS LIKE JAY CAN BE GROWING SPIRITUALLY IN PRISON, BUT WHEN THEY GET OUT, THEY NEED SOMEONE TO TAKE THEM BY THE ELBOW AND LEAD THEM.

—mentor Niels

I'M MAKING IT OUT IN THE WORLD. BUT WHEN IT GETS A LITTLE DARK, I KNOW THAT NIELS IS THERE. HE'S AN ANCHOR FOR ME.

—ex-prisoner Jay

JAY AND NIELS:
BONDED BY THE
LOVE OF CHRIST.

AN EX-PRISONER

SUPPORT GROUP MEETS

TO ENCOURAGE EACH

OTHER AND TALK ABOUT

THE CHALLENGES OF

LIFE OUTSIDE PRISON.

IT'S EASIER TO MINISTER INSIDE A PRISON. YOU KNOW YOU CAN COME
OUT. BUT ONCE THEY'RE OUT THERE AND YOU GET INVOLVED WITH THEM,
THEY CAN BE A FULL-TIME CHALLENGE. THAT'S WHERE THE CHURCH HAS
TO PARTICIPATE AS A BODY BECAUSE YOU CAN'T EXPECT ONE FAMILY OR
ONE PERSON TO TAKE IT ON.

—*PFM volunteer*

In Community Service Projects (CSP), furloughed prisoners prepare for parole work alongside volunteers—tangibly rejuvenating communities infested by crime.

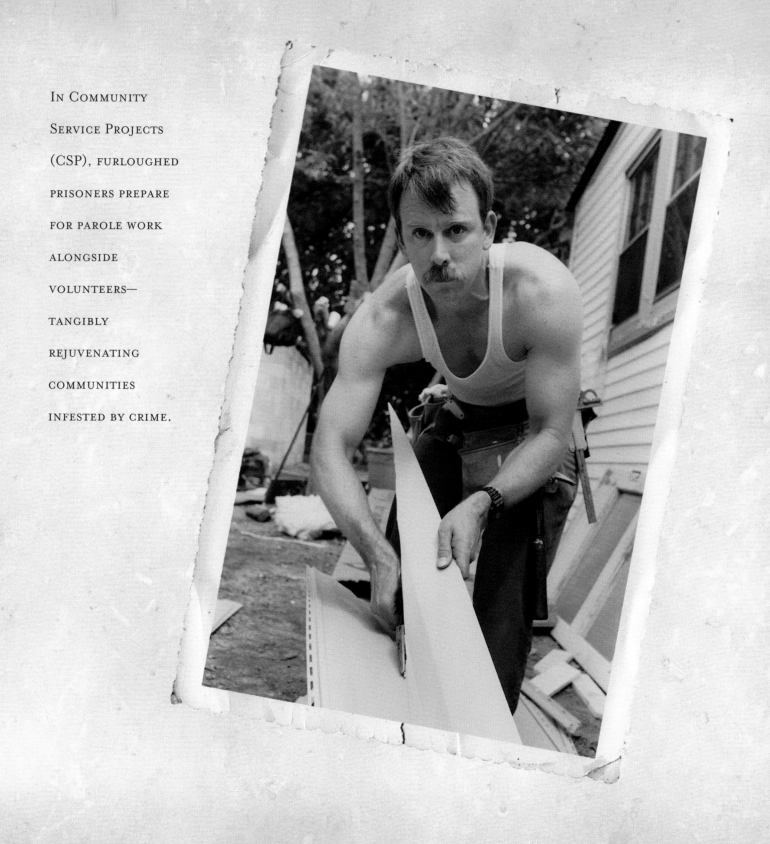

IN 1995 TWENTY-
THREE COMMUNITY
SERVICE PROJECTS
TOOK PLACE ACROSS
THE UNITED STATES.

When Jim Boyd—convicted of armed robbery of John and Helen Wilsons' pharmacy—went back to the scene of the crime, he gained a new understanding of his victims' pain: "Mrs. Wilson told me that she lived in fear every time a stranger walked in the door of the pharmacy. That robbery really affected her."

John Wilson reflects, "The victim is never properly compensated for what happens to him. Those young men came in here and robbed us at gunpoint; they went to prison, but that nervous tension associated with [the holdup] will never go away."

Although John readily accepted Jim's reconciling gestures, he admits, "I still hear the click [of the gun] every once in a while!"

MATCHPOINT PAIRS ADULT CHRISTIAN MENTORS WITH YOUTH AT RISK OF BECOMING CHRONIC OFFENDERS. RESEARCH SHOWS THAT MATCHPOINT YOUTHS RECIDIVATE AT ONLY ONE-SIXTH THE RATE OF OTHER YOUTHS WITH SIMILAR CRIMINAL AND CONFINEMENT HISTORIES: 11 PERCENT COMPARED WITH 66–70 PERCENT (OPPOSITE PAGE RIGHT).

WELL, MY [MENTOR] HAS HELPED ME A LOT. I USED TO BE A WILD PERSON. HE HELPED ME LEARN ABOUT GOD, AND MY LIFE HAS BEEN CHANGED.

—*mentored youth*

VII A Hand to Hold

FROM DEATH ROW SEMINARS THAT PREPARE THOSE ON DEATH ROW FOR

THEIR IMPENDING DEATH TO BEFRIENDING A PRISONER SUFERING WITH AIDS,

PRISON FELLOWSHIP MINISTRIES REACHES OUT TO THOSE ON THE EDGE OF LIFE.

When PFM volunteer Bob McAlister first met inmate Rusty Woomer, cockroaches had infested Rusty's filthy cell and were crawling freely across his body. But then Bob introduced Rusty to Jesus Christ. The result: a clean spiritual slate and an immaculate prison cell. During Rusty's last four and a half years, Bob, while working for the governor of South Carolina, spent hundreds of hours visiting his death-row friend.

Easter weekend [1990] Chuck Colson visited South Carolina's death row, where he discovered two brothers in Christ facing their imminent good-byes. Ronald Woomer was sentenced to die in two weeks; PFM volunteer Bob McAlister was standing with him in his last days. Bob, deputy chief of staff for the governor of South Carolina, shares his friend's story—of God's saving grace.

The condemned man sat on the edge of a bed, his freshly shaven head and right leg glistening with a thin coat of a conducting gel to aid the transmission of two thousand volts of electricity through his body. "Paps," he told me, "the only thing I ever wanted was a home. Now I'm about to get one."

Not more than a score of minutes later on April 27, Ronald Rusty Woomer, thirty-five years old, killer of four innocent people in one of South Carolina's most notorious murder sprees, died in this state's electric chair.

It happened eight days ago. I am writing this article at Prison Fellowship's request, and I do so reluctantly for several reasons. First, the memories of the last days, hours, and seconds with the man who was as close as a son still ache like fresh wounds. Second, Rusty's

case stirred bitter passions throughout South Carolina. I know that I will be criticized for writing about the killer, not the victims. Third, others will question my not using this article as a forum to denounce capital punishment.

But I agreed to write this article for one reason: to exalt the life-changing power of the Lord Jesus Christ in a

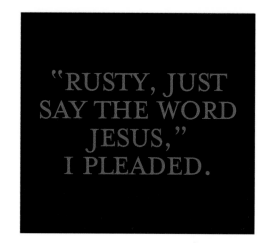

"RUSTY, JUST SAY THE WORD JESUS," I PLEADED.

man who committed senseless, brutal crimes. God's grace is the focus, His grace in a man who, like the rest of us, did not deserve it but accepted that which was freely given. "By grace you have been saved, through faith—and this not from yourselves, it is the gift of God—not by works, so that no one can boast."

Columbia, South Carolina, was resplendent in hues of orange and red on a chilly October night in 1985 outside

the century-old Central Correctional Institution. But the magnificent autumnal finery gave way to bleak grays in cell block 2, better known as death row, where convicted killers waited to die.

I had known Jesus as my Lord for just over a year and had been visiting death row as a volunteer for Prison Fellowship for just under a year.

Late in the evening, as I walked up to the last cell, I saw a sight I will never forget: Rusty, his face the color of chalk, sitting on the floor—motionless. Crawling aimlessly like so many drunks, dozens of roaches covered the walls and floor. But what froze my soul were the roaches crawling on the man—his lap, his shoulders—and such was his despair that he did not flick them off.

I sat down on the floor and tried to talk to him. He could not talk back. He just stared. It was a perfect picture of sin: filthy, degrading, and hopeless. In vain I tried to rouse a response. Frustrated and scared, I prayed aloud that God would cut through the evil in that cell and pierce the heart of its inhabitant.

"Rusty, just say the word *Jesus*," I pleaded.

With much effort, he pursed his lips together and whispered, "Jesus."

"Just look at you," I gently chided.

"Your cell's filthy and so are you. The roaches have taken over, and you're spiritually a dead man, Son. Jesus can give you something better."

I asked Rusty if he wanted to accept Jesus as his Lord and Savior. Through tears, he nodded, then prayed. "Jesus, I've hurt a lot of people. Ain't no way that I deserve You to hear me. But I'm tired and I'm sick and I'm lonely. My mama's dead, and she's in heaven with You, and I never got to tell her 'bye. Please forgive me, Jesus, for everything I've done. I don't know much about You, but I'm willing to learn, and I thank You for listening to me."

I went back to see him the following Monday. I walked up to his cell; it was spotless. Gone were the dirt and roaches and porno magazines. The walls were scrubbed, the bed was made, and the scent of disinfectant hung in the air.

"Bob, how do you like it?" exclaimed a smiling, energized Rusty. "I spent all weekend cleaning out my cell 'cause I figured that's what Jesus wanted me to do."

"Rusty," I blurted, "it took all weekend to clean out your cell, but it took Jesus an instant to clean out your life."

Rusty and I became brothers in Christ. He loved to sit and listen as I read the Bible. During these quiet times of Bible reading, talking, and praying over four and a half years, I hope I taught Rusty something about living. He taught me about dying.

As his appeals were turned down and his execution became a certainty, Rusty developed a simple vision of the hereafter: "When I get to heaven, Jesus and my mama are gonna be waitin' for me,"

> "WHEN I GET TO HEAVEN, JESUS AND MY MAMA ARE GONNA BE WAITIN' FOR ME."

he would say in his thick West Virginia drawl. "And my mama and me are gonna go fishin'."

Going fishin' with Mama. This was Rusty's picture of heaven, and I later learned why. According to court documents and my own discussions with those familiar with his background, Rusty's childhood was one of poverty and abuse. He lived under bridges and in restrooms in his teen years. According to a report published shortly before his execution, "Income from Woomer's father was first spent on alcohol, followed by food for hunting dogs and then food for the children."

Rusty clung to the vision of going fishing with his mother because it was one of his few good childhood memories. He wrote shortly before his death, "I not once ever saw her get a new pair of shoes or new dress or anything new, not even on Christmas. . . . When she died . . . I was crying because I knew she was in heaven . . . and I knew nothing could ever hurt her or do bad things to her again."

Rusty never used childhood poverty and abuse as an excuse for his murderous rampage. He grew to understand sin and individual accountability and constantly laid his sins at the cross.

Despite the certainty of God's forgiveness, Rusty was haunted by his crime, tormented by the hurt and suffering he had caused. "If my death will bring peace to the people I've hurt so bad, then it's time for me to die," he said of the victims' families just hours before his death.

Then last summer he received a letter from Lee Hewitt, the younger brother of Della Louise Sellers, for whose murder Rusty was to be executed. It was a letter of forgiveness. Lee described his life of sin and how the

Lord had entered his life after his sister's murder. "The Bible says Jesus won't forgive us unless we forgive others," Lee later said. "Rusty and I are now brothers in Christ, and I had no choice but to forgive him. I love him."

Though Lee's family did not initially support his reconciling efforts, he chose to live out his faith. Twelve days before Rusty's execution, I took Lee and his wife, Barbara, to meet Rusty for the first and only time. There were tears in everyone's eyes as Rusty said, "What you have done made God's Word complete for me." Lee's forgiveness personified the forgiveness Rusty had already received from Christ.

Seventy-two hours before execution, state law requires that the condemned be taken from death row to the death house, or, in less stark terminology, the capital punishment facility. The execution was scheduled for one o'clock on Friday morning.

Rusty spent the last three days of his life stripped of his possessions, confined to a clinically clean cell about thirty paces from the electric chair. Under around-the-clock surveillance by a contingent of guards, he never had a moment free of scrutiny. A nurse routinely stopped to make sure his vital signs were good, the ultimate irony.

Within the confines of rigid death-house regulations, the guards made Rusty's last days as comfortable as possible. For most of society, the death penalty is an abstract concept. Only the prison officials get their hands dirty in an execution. They were real pros; only their eyes betrayed their calm demeanor as the seconds ticked off.

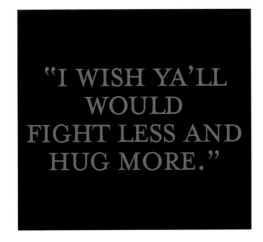

"I WISH YA'LL WOULD FIGHT LESS AND HUG MORE."

It was 3:58 P.M. Thursday, nine hours before Rusty was to die. His father, two sisters, and brother had been visiting him all day. Now it was time for final farewells. As his sisters and brother sobbed and his father stood stone-faced, Rusty gathered them together. "I wish ya'll would fight less and hug more."

Then Rusty asked everyone to bow heads as he led in prayer: "Our pre-

cious Lord, I'm not crying 'cause I feel bad, but 'cause I'm happy. I'm gonna be with You, and You've done everything for me far beyond what I ever deserve. I ask You to watch over my family and take the hurt and sadness from their hearts. I pray that all of this pain and sufferin' will be gone, and I just praise You with all of my heart."

With that prayer Rusty looked at his father, patted his stomach, and joked, "You need to lose some of that, Pappy."

When Rusty's family left, he and I were alone.

It was 7:21 P.M. Rusty was emotionally exhausted from a day of final good-byes, ministering to everyone he talked with, never losing composure. I lay on his bed, and he sat in a chair as the last ray of daylight he would ever see faded through the window. We existed in silence for about twenty minutes until he broke it. "Ya know, Paps, I feel real happy. I just want to go on home now. I don't want to stay here; things are just too bad down here. I just feel real peaceful, and I know Mama's waitin' on me up there."

The Holy Spirit was doing His final work in Rusty's life—and further work in mine. As we sat there, the peace of God washed over us both—a peace that I cannot begin to describe. In that darkened, quiet cell after a frenetic day of emotional upheaval, God chose to move in our hearts, replacing the burdens and fears with the majestic assurance that Rusty would break away from the body of sin and suffering and be whisked away to heaven.

I don't think I will ever be the same.

At 11:45 P.M. I accompanied Rusty to the preparation room. I sat at his feet as a Department of Corrections barber, surrounded by a dozen officials, began the grotesque process of shaving his head and right leg. "Paps," he said, "read me the Bible one last time."

I opened my Bible to Revelation 21:4, the description of the new heaven and earth. As the electric razor hummed, I read, "He shall wipe away every tear from their eyes; and there shall no longer be any death; there shall no longer be any mourning, or crying, or pain" (NASB).

A clump of Rusty's hair fell on my lap; another clump fell on my Bible. I looked up, and with a half-shaven head, Rusty was smiling—a peaceful smile that I have never seen on another human being. I do not know his thoughts, but they were the thoughts of a man who was not afraid of death. At 12:55 A.M. they came to get Rusty. After reading him the death warrant, Warden George Martin asked, "Rusty, are you ready?"

"Let's go," he replied.

I followed Rusty to the death chamber, and my final words to him were, "Rusty, look to Jesus."

Rusty was strapped into the chair, a leather strap over his right leg and a leather helmet attached to his head. I heard his last words: "I'm sorry. I claim Jesus Christ as my Savior. My only wish is that everyone in the world could feel the love I have felt from Him."

Rusty's body died at 1:05 A.M. But I am convinced that he and his mama are fishin' in heavenly streams.

BOB McALISTER
From the July 1990 issue of JUBILEE

LONELINESS CAN
STRIKE HARD IN
PRISON. MANY
INMATES NEVER
RECEIVE MAIL OR
VISITS FROM
FRIENDS OR FAMILY.

THANK YOU FOR TAKING PAINS TO SEE THE HURT LITTLE BOY

INSIDE THIS MEAN MAN. PRAY FOR THE HEALING OF THIS

"LITTLE BOY."

—a prisoner

Philip cringes as he pulls his right foot toward him and kneads it gently. "It feels like a hammer is pounding it," he says weakly. Despite the room's stuffy heat, he wears blue socks covered with tiny fuzz balls.

Like the socks, the hospital walls have seen better days. Flattened Venetian blinds cast shadows across patches of white showing through peeling pink paint.

"I like to watch wrestling," says Philip as he clicks off the television to greet us, his Saturday-morning visitors. "It reminds me of how strong I used to be." Now his withered body wouldn't even qualify for featherweight status. AIDS has taken care of that.

Philip's prison term doesn't end until sometime in the next century, but he has a chance for parole before the end of the year—if his body can hold out that long. "All I want is to see my four-year-old daughter before I die," he says. Doctors have given him six months.

Recently Philip was ready to sacrifice even that, when the horror of AIDS goaded him toward suicide. But Christ's love touched him—just as two thousand years ago it touched the untouchable leper—and Philip now knows that, despite medical predictions, God has given him eternity.

That hope lights his face with a smile as motherly Prison Fellowship volunteer Miriam Robinson sings a familiar children's hymn, her words slightly muffled by a starched hospital mask. The corners of his eyes sparkle with tears as Miriam inserts his name: "Yes, Jesus loves Philip." Unobtrusively, volunteer partner Paulet Cooke slips

> "ALL I WANT IS TO SEE MY FOUR-YEAR-OLD DAUGHTER BEFORE I DIE."

on a pair of sterilized gloves and gently wipes clean Philip's tray stand.

Minutes later, two doors down the hall, volunteer coordinator Adrienne May and I introduce ourselves to Lenny, a new patient. When Adrienne tells him we're Christians, Lenny's hands spring up to cover the tears that gush down his cheeks. "I just accepted Christ two weeks ago, and I'm fifty-four years old," he sobs. "What took me

so long?" It is the pained cry of one who knows his life is at its last lap, yet he assures us his tears are of joy—that God has forgiven and accepted him.

I take his limp hand and cradle it in mine. "God sent you to me," he says to both of us.

In the Shadow of Death

Every Saturday Adrienne and her team of PFM volunteers come from various New York burroughs and suburbs to visit Saint Clare's Hospital in the crime-ridden "Hell's Kitchen" neighborhood of Manhattan. For three hours, behind the locked and guarded doors of the prisoner AIDS ward, they hold weakened hands, help change soiled bedding, fetch cups of soothing ice chips, read the comforting Word of God—and do whatever is needed to show Christ's love to men and women in the shadow of death.

"One July I had a patient die every week," says Adrienne, who has visited Saint Clare's for more than four years. "Sometimes it's very, very hard. But I can't imagine being anyplace else on Saturdays."

Adrienne, like many of the team, came to Saint Clare's via other PFM programs. For years she led Bible studies at Bayview Correctional Facility;

TERMINALLY ILL AIDS
patients find solace
in Adrienne May's
expressions of God's
compassionate care.

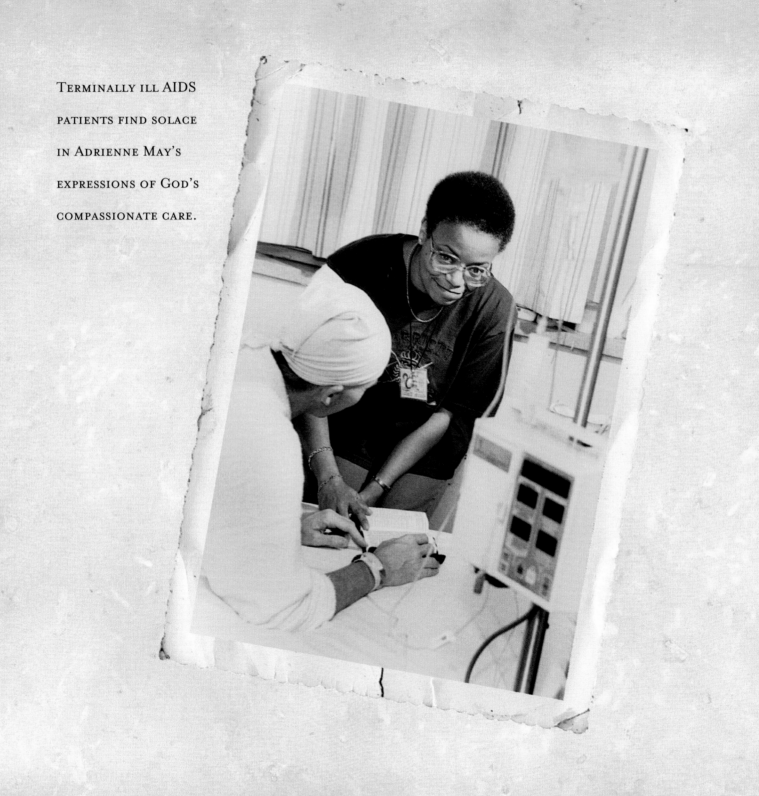

"EITHER WE TRUST THE LORD OR WE DON'T," SAYS ADRIENNE. "AND HE HAS REALLY PROTECTED US."

then several female prisoners asked her to visit their fellow inmates with AIDS. Her occasional trips to Saint Clare's soon became a regular ministry.

Paulet and Miriam wanted to "do more" with PFM after participating in Angel Tree and gravitated to the AIDS ministry when they learned of it earlier this year. "After I received Jesus into my heart, God gave me a love for those nobodies that nobody wants," says Miriam, a teacher and a Christian for many years. She speaks of the male patients with a mother's tenderness: "They may have a macho hardness, but inside they're just little boys crying out for help." Perhaps that is why so many respond with tears to her gentle songs of Jesus.

For Darnell Harris, also active in PFM prison Bible studies, the push to AIDS ministry came from Jesus' words in Matthew 25:35-36: "For I was hungry, and you gave Me something to eat; I was thirsty, and you gave Me drink; I was a stranger, and you invited Me in; naked, and you clothed Me; I was sick, and you visited Me; I was in prison, and you came to Me" (NASB).

"Matthew 25 is about serving," Darnell summarizes. "That's what God's kingdom is about."

"These are broken people, and they need to know somebody cares," says Addis Williams, who had already spent several years ministering to terminally ill patients at another New York hospital when he started visiting Saint Clare's three years ago. At first the white, professional puppeteer from Louisiana questioned whether he could effectively reach out to the primarily minority,

> "THEY MAY HAVE A MACHO HARDNESS, BUT INSIDE THEY'RE JUST LITTLE BOYS CRYING OUT FOR HELP."

streetwise prisoners. "But Adrienne told me, 'You've got no idea the impact you'll have on people who have always felt the white man couldn't care less about them.' After that I relaxed."

During visits the volunteers take the precautions posted on the patients' doors: Hospital masks and sometimes gloves are required with those in "respiratory isolation" or afflicted with related diseases such as tuberculosis. "But the bottom line," says Adrienne, "is either we trust the Lord or we don't. And He has really protected us."

Adrienne's unflinching faith astonished PFM Area Director Ken Ball, who recalls a time he accompanied her to the room of a heavily medicated patient. "Adrienne got cups of orange juice for both herself and the patient. Somehow their cups got crossed, and she began drinking out of his. When she noticed the mistake, she gently said to the man, 'Oh, I'm sorry. I drank from your orange juice.' Others would have run to the bathroom and thrown up out of panic. But Adrienne did not skip a beat in her ministry to him."

No Sugarcoating

It's close to noon as we round the corner and enter Roger's room. He chooses the milk and lemon-lime soda from his lunch tray and pushes the rest aside. "I really feel crummy today," he tells Adrienne, knowing she doesn't expect a sugarcoated synopsis. The assorted medications all come with their own array of side effects: headaches, nausea, diarrhea, blurred vision. He leans back against the pillow and cocks his head to one side so he can see out of his good eye. He wants to sleep, and yet he doesn't want Adrienne to leave.

An advertisement comes on the television, and Roger immediately identifies the background music as that of Aaron Copland. Back in the Midwest he sang professionally, and when I tell him I'm just starting to listen to opera, he tutors me in the differences between Bizet's entertaining intensity and Wagner's psychological intrigue. He and Adrienne, also a musician, trade comments on favorite productions. "You've probably sung this," she tells him, reading a passage from the Psalms. He recalls the lines; the message has not yet entered his heart. Still, he looks forward to Adrienne's weekly visits and welcomes her dry wit that matches his own. "You make me laugh," he praises sincerely. "That's really something!"

"Some people are incredibly open to the gospel at the very first visit; for some it takes a while," Adrienne later explains. "And some never open up. That's hard, especially when you know they are going to die. But we have to accept that however earnestly we might hope for someone to be saved, even Jesus lets them say no."

Since only God can know "the state of the heart," adds Paulet, "we keep going with the message of hope because God is a deliverer."

That truth is evident in Philip's smile, in Lenny's tears. No matter how much time is left for these desperately ill prisoners, God has called them to spend eternity with Him. Though the

> ## THOUGH THE DESTINATION IS PRECIOUS, THE JOURNEY IS PAINFUL AND HARD.

destination is precious, the journey is painful and hard.

The compassionate presence of the PFM volunteers helps ease some of that pain. As a grateful Philip told one of them, "I hope when it is your time to die, you will have someone to hold your hand the way you are holding mine."

BECKY BEANE
From the November 1994 issue of JUBILEE

SAINT CLARE'S SITS IN HELL'S KITCHEN, A HOTBED FOR DRUG DEALERS. BUT ON SATURDAYS, SAY PFM VOLUNTEERS, THERE'S NO PLACE THEY'D RATHER BE (FULL PAGE RIGHT).

VIII | A Circle of Grace

AFTER A PRISONER DISCOVERS THE JOY OF A NEW

LIFE IN CHRIST, HIS OR HER LIFE IS NEVER THE SAME.

SERVING CHRIST BECOMES THE HEART'S DESIRE.

Growing up in Niagara Falls, Charlie Cowart knew about power—the never-ending thunder of Lake Erie squeezed and plummeting over a 185-foot cliff. As a young man, he helped build and then maintain the free world's largest hydro-electric power plant.

The oldest of ten well-disciplined, churchgoing children, Charlie knew about responsibility. When his father died, sixteen-year old Charlie quit school and took a full-time construction job to support the family—and not because his mother asked him to. "It was just something I felt strongly about," he says.

When Charlie married at age twenty-one, his wife, Emma, felt strongly about Charlie getting his high school equivalency diploma, "I was too busy," he says. Supporting two families. Working two jobs. "But she kept after me till I got so annoyed that I signed up" and easily passed the exam. Time has a way of changing one's perspective. Looking back, soft-spoken Charlie says, "I'm so grateful for her encouragement at that point."

For some thirty years, as he raised his four children and actively served his local church, Charlie made the work ethic work. Moonlighting at Niagara University led to tenure as campus security director. Then in 1971 he accepted a bigger challenge as an officer—corporate security director—of a large bank.

But in Buffalo the good life turned sour. "I became embittered," admits Charlie, referring to his transfer, or demotion, to manager of the mail room and messenger services for supposed health reasons. It's hard for him to talk about the subsequent events leading up to his 1983 indictment for embezzlement. "I justified what I did; it was my

> ## "NOTHING JUSTIFIED WHAT I DID," HE SAYS QUIETLY.

way of getting back for having been treated unfairly." Again, Charlie's perspective has changed with time. "Nothing justified what I did," he says quietly.

When confronted with convicting evidence, Charlie couldn't face Emma. "I didn't tell her for two or three days. Then my spirit was totally broken, totally. The media played it up—to make an example, I'm sure. I had violated a trust. The consequences of my actions became very vivid. I lost everything—but my family."

And his family stuck by him. "Emma never brought my offense up to me in a negative way," he says, though the consequences created permanent hardship: She had to find work. She got up every morning knowing she and Charlie would spend the rest of their lives paying off restitution and tax debts. Twice a month with son Chuck Jr. she rode eight hours each way to visit Charlie—incarcerated.

There are no barbed-wire fences or foreboding stone walls at a minimum-security federal prison camp, yet a spirit-shackled man moved into the Danbury dormitory: A disillusioned, fearful Charlie wanted lawyers to appeal; he wanted out; he wanted heaven and earth to shake with the power of Niagara Falls.

But he found his freedom and God's power where he least expected it—on the walking paths of that prison camp. "Walking became an avocation," he says. "You walk and you talk and you pray. And during one of those times I gave it over to the Lord—my sin, my fear. I sought His forgiveness and received His peace."

Charlie found another surprise in Danbury. A Prison Fellowship Bible study and seminar program led by Connecticut/Rhode Island Area Director Bob Wollenweber and volunteers Charlie feels indebted to: "Bob's wife, Wilma; Carol Salka, who mentored, encouraged, and befriended me; Joan Kevins;

At a recent In-Prison Seminar
at Attica Correctional Facility, in one discussion
group all eyes were on Charlie, PFM area director for western New York.

and Andrew and Kathy Agemy. I could go on and on. A loving body of Christians reached out to us. Churches in Connecticut were writing my wife. On occasion a missions group would send a check to her."

Assigned a kitchen job that provided "down time" between meals, Charlie spent his time studying God's Word and encouraging fellow Christians. Seeing Charlie's commitment and leadership potential, Wollenweber and Chaplain Buff Graham recommended that he be furloughed to attend PFM's two-week Washington Discipleship Seminar.

The camp superintendent laughed when Charlie asked for the February 1985 furlough. "He told me there was no way an inmate was going to go out and attend a discipleship seminar." But further negotiations softened his position. Charlie could go if he agreed to use the leadership training to lighten the chaplain's load.

"The WDS had a powerful impact on me. Webster doesn't define what I brought away from the seminar," says Charlie, who never got to keep his agreement with the superintendent. Less than a month after the seminar, Emma called sobbing with the good news that the judge had reduced Charlie's sentence. He was a free man.

Danbury's loss was to become New York's gain, for in January 1986 Charlie joined the PFM staff as area director of the western half of the state. With the self-knowledge that comes with age, he humbly acknowledges the obvious: "People are my forte."

And Chaplain Jeff Carter of Attica Correctional Facility—one of sixteen state penal institutions in Charlie's area—

> ## "WEBSTER DOESN'T DEFINE WHAT I BROUGHT AWAY FROM THE [DISCIPLESHIP] SEMINAR."

agrees: "Charlie has a way of showing an interest in people without putting himself in the forefront. You can see that he totally enjoys working with people."

Walk into PFM's western New York office on Grand Island in the middle of the Niagara River, and you'll be greeted by Charlie's gentle smile that cannot quite hide a trace of sorrow: In August 1988 his faithful Emma left his side, having suffered a fatal stroke.

Confident that Emma is walking streets of gold, Charlie still renews his strength by talking to his Lord while walking footpaths—now within sight and sound of what the locals call The Falls. And very occasionally he enjoys a few minutes of fishing.

Fishing—in the Niagara River? When asked, Charlie says yes, God's wonderfully made fish can survive the 185-foot plunge, making their way to the still waters of Lake Ontario.

You believe what Charlie says about the fish because he's lived here for more than half a century.

Charlie doesn't talk about freshwater fish for long, for he has more important topics on his mind. "A lot of cynics out in the world don't believe a person's life can be changed in prison. But one of the great joys of this work is seeing God's handiwork in changing those lives.

"As an area director I've learned that we're just fishers of men. We can throw out the line—recruit and train volunteers, set up Bible studies, match mentors—but there's nothing we as humans can do to guarantee results. It's the Lord's ministry. We're called to be faithful to the work, but He brings the increase"—the fishing nets full and breaking.

EVELYN BENCE
From the September 1991 issue of JUBILEE

While incarcerated in a Missouri federal prison, Ken Jackson jerked awake one night to see an apparently drug-crazed inmate ready to bludgeon him with a golf club. "I didn't know what to do," says Ken, despite his claim to several Golden Glove boxing trophies. "So I just stared at him and finally said, 'Well, either use the club, or you're going to wear it.'" The inmate darted off, leaving Ken to toss fitfully the rest of the night.

"In prison, you just never knew who you were dealing with," says Ken, recalling another prison story: Several years later, as a staff member with Prison Fellowship, Ken leaped in to avert seeming disaster in the last moments of a PFM seminar. For five days a particular prisoner had threatened and heckled the PFM volunteers and seminar participants. Ken had been warned that he was "the rottenest guy you ever saw"—head pimp of an inmate prostitution ring.

So at the closing altar call, when the inmate lunged toward the seminar instructor, Ken rushed forward, thinking, *I've got to save him!* But when Ken got to the front, "that big guy had picked [the instructor] right off the floor and said, 'Herman, if there's anything truthful about this Jesus Christ you have been talking about all week, I want Him, and I want Him right now!' With tears running

down his face, the guy received Christ that day. It just blew my mind!"

After more than seventeen years as a Prison Fellowship staffer, big, bold Ken Jackson can share a litany of stories about the challenges of ministry; the memorable, miraculous moments that prove "There is hope for sinners, whether or not they be prisoners."

> "I JUST COULDN'T COMPREHEND THAT I WAS IN COURT HAVING TO DEFEND MYSELF FOR SOMETHING I DIDN'T DO."

Ken's own entry into prison came unexpectedly in the mid-1970s. A self-avowed "hardworking guy" who "liked to get things done without messing around," he had racked up a series of successes as a farmer, amateur boxer, World War II aerial gunner, traveling salesman, and business entrepreneur.

Ken also liked to get things done honestly—a trait that not all his employees similarly prized. When a colleague in

his land-development company took some unethical "shortcuts," Ken's CEO status dragged him into fraud and conspiracy charges.

"I just couldn't comprehend that I was in court having to defend myself for something I didn't do," Ken remembers. Even the panache of Ken's famous attorney, F. Lee Bailey, couldn't save him. His conviction brought three years in federal prison.

The Coming of "Colson's People"
The day he walked into the facility at Springfield, Missouri, in 1976 "was the most horrible day of my life," says Ken, recalling the experience and the unleashed humiliation. Two prison guards grabbed him by the arms and whisked him into a room, where "they stripped me down and examined every cavity in my body. Then they gave me a number and told me to remember it because that was now my name."

Immediately assigned to kitchen duty, Ken "sat there and cried half the night. I was thinking about my wife, about the doors clanging shut behind me, about not being able to go home. I was afraid of everybody around me; I didn't know who they were, what they were. I was afraid to close my eyes."

But Ken found solace in his long held

faith in Christ. "When I went to prison, I made a commitment to the Lord that whatever He called me to from then on, that would be my life. I just wanted to be in His will and in some way be a minister."

That prayer was answered ninety days later when "Chuck Colson's people showed up" to select two Christian inmates to attend Prison Fellowship's new Washington Discipleship Seminar. Less than a year old, PFM didn't yet take its seminars into prison; instead, low-security federal prisoners were furloughed to the nation's capital for two weeks of training "to be ambassadors for Christ" back in their prison. After extensive interviews at Springfield, the PFM reps chose Ken.

"I gained so much in those two weeks, I can't believe it!" says Ken, losing none of his original enthusiasm in nineteen years. During the day the furloughed prisoners grappled with principles and practices of Christian leadership; at night they shared their testimonies in local churches.

The men also received some unconventional practice in frontline evangelism: One day the PFM trainers took them to a Washington, D.C., prison: "They lined us up in front of the cells, and said, 'Go ahead and witness.'" Ken took one look at the hulking prisoner in front of him and thought, *I don't want to talk to this guy. I want to get out of here!* But Ken was soon chatting about his own life as a prisoner and his relationship with Christ. "When I finally got into it, I really got excited," says Ken.

God's Gift of Hope
Back at Springfield, Ken's zeal motivated him immediately to start and promote a

> **"THEY LINED US UP IN FRONT OF THE CELLS, AND SAID, 'GO AHEAD AND WITNESS.'"**

Tuesday morning prayer meeting. That first day Ken, the chaplain, and a fellow PFM seminar graduate gathered in the prayer room at seven. "There wasn't anybody else there," Ken recalls. "So we just stood there and prayed. And by the time we turned around and looked, the place was filling up!" Nearly seventy men came out to pray.

One of those was Junior, recently transferred to Springfield to have a tumor removed in the prison hospital. The impending surgery "was our first prayer request," explains Ken. "We prayed for Junior. The next Tuesday he was back at the prayer meeting—declared cured with no operation! The doctors didn't know what happened!"

But Junior's prayer partners knew. "It was as if God said, 'Here is a bunch of prisoners with no hope. I think I'll give them a little,'" says Ken.

Ken's hope in Christ sustained him through twenty-one months of prison life, beginning at Springfield and ending at a Chicago facility. Then on December 5, 1977, Ken walked out a free man. "It was one of the biggest snowstorms ever, and they dressed me in a summer leisure suit!" he says, snickering. Downed phone lines kept him from calling his wife in Fort Wayne, Indiana. A wreck on the tracks forced his train to take an hourslong detour. "But I didn't care," he remembers. "I was headed home!"

When he got to the Fort Wayne train station, however, no taxis or buses could get through to take him the last leg of his trip. So Ken struck out on foot, managing to get three miles before the subzero temperature and his soaked deck shoes forced him into a warm tavern. Finally, getting his grown son on the phone and convincing him that his father really was

MOST OBSTACLES TO PRISON MINISTRY ARE NO MATCH FOR KEN'S BULLDOG TENACITY. "IF SATAN THREW UP A WALL," SAYS ONE VOLUNTEER, "KEN MADE A DOOR."

DURING KEN JACKSON'S PRISON STINT, PFM'S PROGRAMS GAVE HIM A ZEAL FOR MINISTRY TO FELLOW PRISONERS THAT CARRIED ON LONG AFTER RELEASE. MINISTRY MEMORIES REMIND HIM THAT "THERE IS HOPE FOR SINNERS, WHETHER THEY BE PRISONERS OR NOT."

AT FIRST KEN WASN'T EXACTLY

EAGER TO SHARE HIS FAITH

WITH ANOTHER PRISONER. "BUT

WHEN I FINALLY GOT INTO IT, I

REALLY GOT EXCITED."

out of prison and needed a ride, Ken made it home in the middle of the night. His eyes water as he remembers his sleepy, unsuspecting wife, Betty Lou, opening the door to him. "It was like another life starting."

Ken wasn't at all interested in going back into prison, "but the Lord was dealing with me," he explains. As Prison Fellowship persistently came to mind, he developed an elaborate outline of how the organization could unite with local churches to minister to prisoners and ex-prisoners. "I sent it to Colson," he says. A few weeks later Ken was on his way east for a job interview.

In April 1978 PFM hired fifty-three-year-old Ken to join its small staff—despite the warning given in a preemployment psychological test. "You should be cautious about hiring this man," Ken paraphrases, "because with his ambition, he probably won't be with you more than three years." Ken's tenure with PFM has reached nearly six times that prediction.

Resurrected Life
Those years have provided "one of the most thrilling parts of my life"—filled with examples of God's transforming power. He recalls a Jewish inmate at a Kansas In-Prison Seminar, whose loud jeers and disruptive questions finally

drove Ken to confront the man's disrespect and challenge him to listen to the instructor. At the end of the seminar, the inmate's only comment on the teaching was that it was "different."

But when Ken returned to the prison six months later, the same inmate ran up and grabbed Ken. "Jackson, it's your fault!" he yelled. "It's your fault I

"PFM WILL ALWAYS BE A PART OF ME."

became a Christian."

Then he presented Ken with a home-made treasure: a cross fashioned from iron nails of the prison's dismantled gallows. A tool of death reborn as an emblem of life.

With a mental scrapbook full of such stories, Ken retired from PFM in June, serving the last five years as overseeing field director in the nine-state Great Lakes region. He'll still volunteer "to do

whatever PFM wants me to do—without all the traveling!" Turning seventy in July, Ken also plans to complete his studies for ordination as a Methodist minister, spend more time with Betty Lou, and maybe even get in a few rounds of golf.

"I think my retiring from PFM is just part of a cycle that needed to be completed," he says. "But I would never walk away from it. I've always considered PFM serious business because, as a prisoner, I received the benefits of it. PFM will always be a part of me."

BECKY BEANE
From the July/August 1995 issue of JUBILEE

The squeeze was tight. On May 16, 1980, 250 refugees from Cuba crowded onto a shrimp boat made to hold 125—maximum. Like most of the other emigrants, thirty-year-old Omar Gonzales had abandoned everything—family, friends, job—to chase the elusive dream of freedom.

The political refugee spent the night retching into the choppy sea, hoping, praying he'd make it to Key West. He'd tried to escape his homeland three times before. Omar knew the ache of defeat. But finally, shortly after dawn, he spotted pelicans on the horizon, then a beach. This was it.

As Omar walked down the gangplank, a uniformed immigration officer handed him a Coca-Cola—as if it were a prize or a symbol of the good life to follow.

That afternoon, Omar and other Marielitos (the 125,000 emigrants who left from the Mariel harbor during the sixty-day boat lift) sat under U.S. government tents, gorging themselves on hot dogs and potato chips. "It was a tremendous feeling of plenteousness," says the Cuban exile. "You could serve yourself as much as you wanted. In my country the food is rationed—it was really a shock."

A few days later, Omar boarded a government plane bound for Fort Chaffee, Arkansas. While in flight, he employed his broken English to translate for the crew and passengers. He was happy to be of service in his new land.

After forty-five days in the Arkansas tent compound, he tracked down and convinced the one American he knew—a bachelor he'd met at a Hemingway fishing tournament—to sponsor him. No longer living under the threat of deport-

> "I WAS MR. ROCKEFELLER. AMERICAN EXPRESS OFFERED ME A $15,000 CREDIT LINE; IT WAS INCREDIBLE."

ment, Omar moved to the Virginia suburbs of Washington, D.C.

Working as a laborer and part-time bartender, Omar soaked in the opulence of the new land. Having subsisted on three-fourths of a pound of meat every nine days and five pounds of rice per month (plus what he could get on the black market), he wandered supermarket aisles in amazement. How could he choose one brand of bread out of twenty?

It was all too much too soon. "I went berserk trying to replace twenty years of communism in one year," says Omar. "Having never been in a democracy, I didn't know how to handle myself."

He especially didn't know how to handle credit cards, the seductive tempters of the good life. They promised the American Dream—the ability to have anything he and his new wife wanted. Having established credit by purchasing two cars, he was courted by MasterCard, Diner's Club, and American Express. He took up their magical offers and charged away his life, enjoying a fancy stereo, expensive jewelry, and lavish vacations. With plastic wands he pursued his idea of freedom—the freedom to feel important.

"I was Mr. Rockefeller," he says. "American Express offered me a $15,000 credit line; it was incredible. When they send you a card like that, you have to use it."

But eventually Omar's dream turned into a nightmare. He visited a fellow immigrant in early 1984 and, overcome with a debt of thousands of dollars, asked how his friend afforded his luxurious lifestyle. The answer? Cocaine.

Convinced it was a harmless drug, Omar began selling and using it. "I used to go to parties where they served

OMAR GONZALES ADMITS HE
DIDN'T KNOW HOW TO HANDLE
THE "PLENTY" HE DISCOVERED
IN THE U.S., THANKS TO
CREDIT CARDS AND COCAINE.

MENTOR JIMMIE MASSIE
(RIGHT) MET OMAR
GONZALES AT A PRISON
FELLOWSHIP SEMINAR.
SINCE OMAR'S RELEASE,
JIMMIE HAS HELPED HIM
GET ON HIS FEET—AND
STAY THERE.

marijuana and cocaine on silver plates. At one point I started believing drugs were legal because they were everywhere." As he became enmeshed in drug dealing, however, Omar realized he was snared in a deadly trap. The people—and their white powder—were dangerous. "Something inside of me was saying, 'Get locked up and get out of this mess.'" When an undercover agent threw him to the ground and stuck a gun to his head, Omar was terrified yet oddly relieved.

Six months after entering the drug world, Omar sat in a county jail staring at a Bible someone had handed him. He remembered his youthful days in the Roman Catholic Church before Castro came to power, and his teenage years handing out tracts for an underground church. "I didn't really know Jesus personally; I just liked the risk." Later, he had lost his university teaching post and narrowly escaped imprisonment for telling one student he thought God had created the world.

Now, as a criminal with his back turned to God, he had been given the outlawed book. "It blew my mind away," says Omar. "I thought if you were a convict, drug dealer, you were of no worth. That Bible symbolized a love I had never experienced."

Feeling deserted by his wife, with no friends or family near, he was lonely. "God, I'm nothing," he said. "Nobody cares about me." A year later, in the fall of 1985, Omar attended a Prison Fellowship In-Prison Seminar (IPS) at a Virginia state prison, where he was serving time. "I was drawn by the poster with people holding hands," he says. "I kept

> ## "THE BIBLE SYMBOLIZED A LOVE I HAD NEVER EXPERIENCED."

seeing those clasped hands, their unity."

At the IPS, Omar met PFM volunteer Jimmie Massie, a stockbroker turned farmer. As their friendship developed through PFM Bible studies and visits, Omar became secure in God's love through His people. "In prison I felt guilty about how much damage I did to teenagers, businessmen—who knows?—but I took all that guilt to Christ and left it there."

Last December [1987] Omar was paroled after serving three years in prison. He was given a change of clothes and $80. "I couldn't have made it without Jimmie or someone with his love, concern, and willingness to risk himself," says Omar. "He and other PFM volunteers gave me capital and a place to live. They provided encouragement when I needed it most."

They also taught him to make—and stick to—a budget. His first two paychecks went toward debts that had been outstanding when he was jailed. The godly discipline Omar learned in prison and the relationship he developed with Jimmie helped him once he gained freedom. This time he could handle its responsibilities. "I learned in prison to trust God for everything, to put Christ first in everything."

Three months out of prison, Omar began teaching high school equivalency classes to prisoners near Richmond. Although ex-prisoners are rarely allowed into prison so soon after release, Jimmie convinced the Department of Corrections (DOC) of Omar's skill and integrity. As one DOC official acknowledged, "Our business is trying to reestablish people in the community, to give them a chance to rebuild their lives. We ought to be right in it ourselves."

Omar was thrilled to be used as Christ's instrument to bring love to a place of great need. "It was a dream come true to go back and let them know through my walk—not my talk—that Jesus remakes you, that you don't have to live in crime."

Omar also got part-time work at a hospital for drug addicts. Having been a prisoner of the state—and of drugs—he commands the respect of those still captive. They capture his heart, for he knows their pain. "I want to empty myself and let Christ use me as an instrument of love.

"Today I can say what I wasn't able to say before: that I am concerned and I love you. I see transfigured faces when I say that. Until Prison Fellowship, nobody ever confronted me and said, 'Omar, I love you.'"

With the help of PFM volunteers, he has secured an apartment and bought a used car. The path has been long and arduous, but God has been there to guide him.

As Omar now celebrates his eighth year in America, he has a new understanding of the land of promise. "America is no longer America where I'm going to be rich," he says. "Today I enjoy people a lot more. And I would like God to use me to reflect His love to other people."

He also better understands liberty. Having lived under communism, where life was threatened, and capitalism, where the pursuit of happiness led to despair, Omar has found true liberty in Christ. "Freedom today," he says, "is the freedom of worship, the freedom of fellowship, and the freedom to express

> **UNTIL PRISON FELLOWSHIP, NOBODY EVER CONFRONTED ME AND SAID, "OMAR, I LOVE YOU."**

myself toward the One who created me. That's real freedom."

ALICE LAWSON SPERAPANI
From the July 1988 issue of Jubilee

TO GOD BE THE GLORY—GREAT THINGS HE HATH DONE!

— Fanny Jane Crosby

In memoriam for their generous testamentary provision to the ministry of Prison Fellowship

Ms. Christine Bruins
Mrs. Marie G. Gillespie
Mr. Walter Griggith
Ms. Mary Findley
Mr. Frank Florik
Mrs. Ruth M. Johnson
Mr. & Mrs. Bob Klanderud
Mrs. Agnes A. Knutsen
Mr. Frank R. Neville
Ms. Hazel Satterthwaite
Mrs. Catherine Schneider
Ms. Genevieve R. Sanders
Mrs. Rose Vickery
Mr. L. Frances Wakefield
Mr. & Mrs. Fred Wheeler

In memoriam for their faithful service on the Board of Directors

Dr. Richard Halverson
Mrs. Rose Totino
Mr. Kenneth T. Wessner

In memoriam for their faithful service as members of the Prison Fellowship Staff

Reverend Herman Heade
Mr. Bob McGuire
Mr. James Murray
Mr. James Whitehead

Anniversary Partners

Virginia Rodner Abbitt
Sharon Abendschoen
W. M. Abney
David & Carol Abraham
Hobie Acker
Greg Ackerson
Bob Adams
Dorothy D. Adams
M. Madeline Adams
Donna M. Adcock
Mr. Rodney J. Addison
Sharlene Agudelo
Mr. & Mrs. Craig R. Ailles
Mr. Stanley Akland
Haig S. Albarian, D.D.S.
Wayne Albin
Margaret & Norris Aldeen
Graydon & Beulah Aldred

Kimberly M. Alexander
Mrs. Arthur Allaire
Carl S. Allee
Anne T. Allen
Lawrence Allen
Linda Kay Allen
Louise Allen
Chuck & Joan Allison
Mr. & Mrs. Kenneth Allison
Mr. & Mrs. John J. Allread
Lucille V. Almond
Ace Alsup Jr.
Rev. & Mrs. Frank Amalfitano
Tom & Elizabeth Amis
Philipp R. Amlinger, M.D.
Richard Amory
Mr. & Mrs. John A. Amos
Drs. Robert & Davida Amsden
Rolf & Doris Amundson
Allen J. Anderson
Andy & Beulah Anderson
Bruce D. Anderson
Carson Anderson Jr.
Mr. & Mrs. Charles M. Anderson
Elizabeth & Carole Anderson
Irene L. Anderson
Mr. & Mrs. Jon Anderson
Karen E. Anderson
Kathy Anderson
Dr. Larry G. Anderson
Lexie Anderson
Ms. Nancy F. Anderson
Tom & Carol Anderson
Ms. Shirley Andexler
Grace Angstadt
Raymond L. Annear
Evelyn Anselevicius
Ida Mae (Wright) Anthony
Miss Kimberly Rose Antigone
Geraldine A. Anzak
Ralph & Karen Appier
Michael & Linda Araujo
H. Taylor Armerding II
Mr. & Mrs. Stan J. Armitage
Nettie L. Armstrong
Robert W. Armstrong
Rose-Marie Armstrong
Camille M. Arnett
Fred D. Arney
Randall & Martha Arnhart
Mrs. Elisabeth Arnold
Fred M. Arnold Jr.
Mary Ann Arnold
Frank & Janet Tanner Arnold
Mr. & Mrs. Randy Arntzen
Mr. & Mrs. Edward F. Arps

Mrs. Margaret Arvin
Alberto Padilla Astacio
G. Marshall Atkins
Aunt Do
Mrs. John W. Austin
Mr. & Mrs. Manuel S. Avila
Rev. & Mrs. S. K. Awoniyi
Mr. & Mrs. John F. Ayers Jr.
Hilda Baab
Henry S. Badeer
Letty A. Baebler
Mr. & Mrs. Timothy Bagot
Catherine J. Bailey
Dr. & Mrs. Joe Weldon Bailey
Mary Anna Bailey
Mrs. Peter Bailey
Mr. & Mrs. Ryland Y. Bailey
Barbara Baker
Mr. & Mrs. George Baker
Isabelle A. Baker
Keith & Gena Baker
Marylou H. Baker
Mrs. Patsy A. Baker
Mr. Randall Baker
Turner & Gretchen Baker
Mr. & Mrs. Richard C. Balben
Harriet L. Baldwin
Gail A. Ball
Margaret Ball
Mr. & Mrs. Walter W. Ballard
Cyndie Balling
Joe M. Bamberg
Mr. & Mrs. Raymond L. Bandy
Mrs. J. J. Banks
Mrs. Shirley D. Banks
Beverly J. Bansemer
Mr. & Mrs. Matthew J. Barany
Paul L. Barber
Dr. & Mrs. Gulio J. Barbero
Frank & Sue Barbian
Ovidiu Bardan
Chris Barker
Mary C. Barker
Mrs. Reva Barkley
Michael J. Barna
Lisa Barnes
Mrs. Olive W. Barnes
Walter I. Barnet
Mrs. Frances Barrett
Jane B. Barrett
Juanita A. Barrett
Norm & Gayla Barstad
Mrs. Violet Bartel
Angeline Basar
Mrs. Marjorie J. Basinger
Rev. Byron W. Bassett

Donald G. Batchelder
Howard & Barbara Bateman
Mrs. Roger E. Bates
Mrs. John P. Batts Sr.
Mr. & Mrs. Cliff Bauer
Lorraine Ruth Bauer
William & Elizabeth Bauer
Royce Ann Bauerlein
Bernice Baugh
Mr. & Mrs. Clyde L. Baugher
Mr. & Mrs. Rick Baughman
Mr. & Mrs. M. C. Bauman
Walter L. Baumann
Mr. Ken Beadle
Mr. & Mrs. Dan L. Beaird
Mrs. Robert L. Beaman Jr.
Richard D. Beard
Mrs. Honor Bearden
Mr. & Mrs. W. G. Beattie
Mr. & Mrs. James D. Beaver
Mr. & Mrs. Henry C. Beck Jr.
Linden & Karen Beck
Richard & Betty Beckett
Catherine R. Bednego
Eldon G. Beer
Lowell & Cindy Beers
Dr. & Mrs. Marc R. Belcastro
S. E. Belcher Jr.
Harry R. Bell
Mavis Currie Bell
Bruce M. Bemis
Mr. Larry S. Bemis
Steven R. Benegar
Mr. & Mrs. Paul V. Benes
Mr. & Mrs. Michael G. Benfer
Dr. & Mrs. John C. Bengtson
Dennis & Linda Bennett
Philip & Marjorie Bennett
Kinuye June Bento
Rick Bergener
Mr. & Mrs. James C. Berger
Grant Bergman
William L. Berkhof
Mrs. Zylpha E. Berlier
Clarence Jerald Berry
Holt & Nola Bertelson
Gary E. Beven, M.D.
Paul A. Beverly
Preston & Joyce Bhang
Dr. & Mrs. Michael W. Bible
James P. Bick
Fred & Virginia Biehler
Dr. & Mrs. James C. Biel
Barbara Bier
Lona Carol Bieter
Mary Jane Billingsley

Mr. & Mrs. Jimmie Bills
B. E. Bilyeu
Mr. & Mrs. Alfred Binder
Patricia Binger
Jeremy & Janet Birdsall
Beulah Bishop
Timothy Bittner
Vernice & Ruth Bixler
Dorothy W. Black
J. Blair
F. J. Ted Blake
Ann L. Blanchet
Floyd Bland
Mr. & Mrs. Robert Blazevich
Anna Mary Blessley
Mark Blevins & Family
Pat E. Bliss
Dr. & Mrs. Lawrence F. Blomberg
James L. Blubaugh
June R. Bluhm
Dora Boah
J. B. Boardman
Robert Boatz
Ione B. Boblitz
Richard E. Bochte
Jennifer J. Bock
Mary Jean Bockbrader
Mr. & Mrs. Rolf Bocker
Clarence C. Bodine
Robert N. Bodwell
Mr. Frank J. Boehme
Herb & Doris Boelens
Wayne & Daphne Boelsma
John & Nancy Boender
Dr. & Mrs. Norm Boeve
Aileen N. Bollinger
Mr. & Mrs. L. A. Bollinger
Paula K. Bolton
Mr. & Mrs. Rodney Bonck Jr.
Al & Mary Jo Bonds
Mr. & Mrs. Wayne L. Bonham
Mr. & Mrs. Robert J. Bonner
Trish Bonnevier
Frank Bono
Roberta Book
Rev. John Booko
Wyleen Boone
Mr. & Mrs. Edwin L. Boote
Beverly H. Booth
Clarence A. Booth
Mrs. Marcella M. Borck
Mr. & Mrs. C. Borgia
Preston Borneman
David S. Bortel
Henry & Jeannie Bosa
Virginia Boteler

MRS. EMILY BOURNE
RAY & ELEANOR BOWDEN
DIANE BOWE
MRS. ANNA MAE BOWMAN
DORIS G. BOWMAN
ESTHER R. BOWMAN
JOHN A. BOWMAN
MARGARET & ELON BOWMAN
TED & BILLIE BOWMAN
MR. & MRS. JEFFREY BOYCE
CHRISTOPHER R. BOYD
ANGELA BOYER
LOIS R. BOYER
MRS. FRANCES L. BOYLE
KAREN BRADFORD
MRS. LEE BRADLEY
NINA BRADLEY
O. D. BRADLEY JR.
MRS. PATRICIA BRADLEY
W. BOLLING BRADLEY
PEGGY BRAMLETT
ROBERT & SHIRLEY BRANCH
REV. & MRS. A. OWEN BRAND
PAUL MANGAN BRANDENBURG
ARTHUR E. BRANDT
DONALD A. BRANDT
JULIUS BRANDT
MR. & MRS. GUY E. BRANHAM
KENNY & HAZEL BRAUN
MR. & MRS. CHARLES BREEDEN
MR. & MRS. BRYAN F. BREFFLE
MR. & MRS. HAROLD L. BREINER
PATRICIA R. BREMER
MR. & MRS. K. SEAN BRENNAN
MR. & MRS. HAROLD D. BRENNEKE
REV. C. E. BRENTLINGER
LEONARD W. BREWER
MELVIN D. BRICKER
EVERETT & SARA BRIDGER
JACK & JOY BRIDGES
W. LLOYD BRIDGES, M.D.
LAURIE BRIERLEY
GLENNA BRIGGS
NORMAN D. BRIGGS
MR. & MRS. ROY BRISTOL
MOTHER ROSA L. BROADOUS
KARL W. BROBERG
CARROLL E. BROCK
DR. & MRS. JOE T. BRODERSON
RAY & LUCILLE BROOKS
STEVEN J. BROOKS
CHARLES & KAY BROWN
CLARENCE W. BROWN
DORIS E. BROWN
E. DEANNE BROWN
FLORENCE BROWN
GEORGE & LEE BROWN
JAMES H. BROWN
JOHN T. BROWN JR.
MR. & MRS. JOSEPH C. BROWN

MELVIN S. BROWN
MR. & MRS. WENDELL E. BROWN
BOB & NORMA BROWNING
ADELE C. BROWNLEE
DON B. BROYLES
MRS. ARLENE BRUBAKER
ROSE E. BRUEGGEMAN
RALPH & AVIS BRUMBAUGH
MRS. LOUISE A. BRUNTZ
BOB & CAROL BRYAN
MR. & MRS. W. B. BRYAN
PAUL & KATIE BRYANT
MR. & MRS. SYDNEY BRYANT
DR. SCOTT C. BUBLIN
RICH & KATHY BUCCHIANERI
JAMES O. BUCHANAN
MRS. NORMA BUCHANAN
F. BUDIWARMAN
BOB & JUNE BUECHNER
THELMA C. BUEHLER
MS. BETTY BUELL
MRS. BUNNY BUHL
PAUL & FRAN BULJAT
CEVERENA H. BUNNEL
MR. & MRS. WALTER BURCHAM
PEYTON D. BURFORD
MRS. DEBRA BURGESS
REV. E. EMANUEL BURKMAN
LORENE BURLEIGH
MS. WANDA M. BURLEIGH
C. P. BURMAN
TOM & KATHY BURNER
LARRY & LINDA BURNEY
MARY BESS BURNS
NORM BURNS
MR. & MRS. ROGER BURNS
JOE & OETHA BURNSIDE
RICHARD E. BURRELL
BARBARA A. BURROWS
MR. & MRS. HARRY BUSBEE
EDWARD & PHYLLIS BUSHOUSE
JAMES & HELENE BUSMAN
CHARLES & EDITH BUTERA
JOANNE BUTGEREIT
IVER O. BUTLER
MARY S. BUTLER
STEVE & GEORGEANN BUTLER
SCOTT BUZBY
ROBERT D. BYERS
PAULA BYHAUG
MR. R. CHARLES BYRAM
KATHERINE H. BYRD
NINA & ED BYRON
WILMA R. CABACUNGAN
STEPHEN W. CABLE
MS. VIOLA S. CAGE
MR. & MRS. J. THOMAS CAINES
WILLIAM & BETH CALABRO
MS. LYDIA CALDERON
ANDREW, MELISSA & BEN CALDWELL

MRS. GRACE JAMES CALDWELL
SUZANNE CALLIHAN
DR. & MRS. KEITH W. CAMERON
DR. & MRS. RUSSELL R. CAMP
MRS. AGNES G. CAMPBELL
MR. & MRS. ALEXANDER CAMPBELL JR.
DONALD S. CAMPBELL
ESTHER M. CAMPBELL
MRS. LORI CAMPBELL
VERA BRUNS CAMPBELL
WAYNE & DAWN CAMPBELL
MR. & MRS. CLIFFORD R. CANTRALL
MR. JESSE CANTU
LOUISE M. CAPRON
ANN CARLISLE
DR. LEE CARLSON
MR. & MRS. RONALD P. CARLSON
MR. & MRS. WAYNE CARLSON
JOE R. CARLTON
MR. & MRS. HOBART M. CARNES
FOREST & DOROTHY CARNINE
MISS KATHRYN E. CARPENTER
MARJORIE CARPENTER
MR. & MRS. ROLLO R. CARR
STEVE & JENNIE CARRELL
MR. & MRS. STEPHEN B. CARROLL
MR. & MRS. GREGORY A. CARSON
MR. & MRS. JAMES R. CARSON
MISS CARY A. CARTER
TINA CARTER
VIRGINIA MILNER CARTER
MR. & MRS. SAMUEL B. CASEY III
MR. & MRS. MIKE CASH
MARLENE A. CASHELL
MRS. ALICE B. CASO
PHYLLIS C. CASSIDY
AMY M. CATES
REV. & MRS. J. HOWARD CATES
JACK & ALICE CAVE
MRS. ANA CAYCE
MRS. JANE VIEH CECIL
LORRAINE E. CEDER
JUDITH CELIS
MRS. GEORGE R. CHADWICK
ULI CHAPA
BILL CHAUSSE
VITUS & CAROL CHENG
MR. & MRS. DAVID W. CHENOT
MAYTIE L. CHERRY
LEE & AGNES CHESTER
MRS. KENNETH CHILDRESS
STEVEN HING-WAN CHIN
SHELDON CHISEN
MR. CHARLES CHOU
MR. & MRS. GREGORY CHRIST
MRS. WESLEY CHRISTENSEN
MARTIN A. CHRISTIAN
CHRISTIAN SINGLES INTERNATIONAL
MR. RAYMOND K. CHRISTIE
MR. & MRS. JOHN D. CHRISTOFF

CLARENCE LEE CHUBB
LEE CHUMBLER
JOHNNY & KATHERINA T. CHUNG
MR. & MRS. PAUL CHURCH
JEAN CHURCHILL
CONNIE M. CIANO
LOUIS & ANITA CICERO
DON CLAIR
MRS. D. S. CLARK
HUGH D. CLARK
JAMES E. CLARK
NORMAN K. CLARK
PAUL & KATHY CLARK
MR. & MRS. EARLE M. CLARKE
JOHN W. CLARKE
CURT & MARGIE CLARKSON
MR. & MRS. PAUL CLAUS
MR. GARY LEE CLAYTON
MR. & MRS. LAWRENCE O. CLAYTON
LES & KAY CLEMENS
PHILIP A. CLEMENS
HERBERT H. CLEMENTS
CINDY & DENNIS CLIFTON
RUTH CLONINGER
LYLE & BETTY CLOVER
REV. & MRS. JAMES COAD JR.
REV. & MRS. DAVID W. COBB
ERNEST L. COBBS
DOLORES L. COCHRAN
MR. & MRS. J. A. COCHRAN JR.
MRS. W. F. COCHRAN
R. L. COCHRANE
PASQUALE D. CODISPOTI
PAMELA CODY
MRS. BOB COEN
TOM & VIRGINIA COLANDREA
HOWARD S. COLE
LISA COLE
RIVERS M. COLE
EVA M. COLEMAN
MARY ELLEN COLEMAN
RICHARD E. COLEMAN
JIM & BECCA COLLINS
LUCILLE P. COLLINS
OPAL H. COLLINS
MR. RAY COLGAN
GLEN W. COLMAN
BILL CONARD
DAVID D. CONDIT
J. RONALD CONDREN
KATHRYN JUNE CONLEY
MR. & MRS. RAY CONN
MR. & MRS. EDWARD CONNELL
MRS. IRA M. CONNER
LEO M. CONNER
MRS. JAMES A. CONNETT
MR. & MRS. WILLIAM H. CONNOR
BRUCE & LORAINE CONSTABLE
JUAN & ANITA CONSTANTINO
CHARLES & MARION CONVER

D. A. COOK
MR. & MRS. KENNETH R. COOK
KIM & KATHRYN COOKE
SARA F. COOKE
JUNE COOPER
JOE COPELAND
LARRY & KAREN COPELAND
HOWARD & MARGARET COPENHAVER
KARILYN J. CORBETT
EUGENE & LOUISE CORBIN
EVELYN CORBIN
MRS. GLORIA CORBIN
MRS. OTTO CORBIN
TIMOTHY H. CORBIN
BILL & ELAINE COREY
DR. & MRS. J. R. CORTNER
CYNTHIA JOHNSON COSBY
JOHN & JUDY COTNER
REV. & MRS. A. COTTO-THORNER
MR. ERNEST COULTAS
N. GRAY COUNTS
MR. & MRS. W. F. COURTRIGHT
ISABEL COUSTEN
CHUCK & CATHY COX
DOUG & SAUNDRA COX
FRANKLIN D. COX
MAXINE COX
OPAL B. COX
MR. & MRS. FRANKLIN COYLE
DAVID L. CRAFT
B. P. CRAIG
DARLENE CRAIG
MRS. HOWARD W. CRAIG
JOHN D. CRAIG
RICHARD & LOUISE CRAIG
DR. RICHARD E. CRAMM
DAVID & CILLA CRANE
NANCY J. CRAVEN
SARAH S. CRAVEN
JOHN CRAYTHORNE
FRANK & MARY CREDENDINO
GILMORE K. CREELMAN
PETER CREFELD
ROBERT A. CRESSMAN JR.
MRS. DOROTHY CREVELING
DAWN E. CRISE
MIKE & SUZANNE CRISP
MR. & MRS. KEN CROCKER
MRS. CAROL G. CRONIN
EDWARD & MARY CROSS
JACK & ARLENE CROSS
MR. & MRS. HOWARD R. CRUGER
MRS. JOHN B. CULVER
BRUCE & PAULINE CUMMINGS
LOIS CUMMINGS
MR. & MRS. MARVIN CUMMINS
RALPH & MABEL CUNNINGHAM
MRS. ROBERT D. CURLEY
MR. & MRS. LEROY S. CURRIER
GREGORY W. CURTICE

Mr. & Mrs. John D. Curtis
Beth H. Cutler
Lillian Tillery Cutrer
Glenn & Janet Dahl
Mr. & Mrs. Mark F. Dahlberg
Corinne & Ina Dahlen
Marilyn Dahlof
Karl E. Dalstad
Sharon & Jim Daly
Norma Eileen Dash
Mr. & Mrs. Rinto Dasuki
Mr. & Mrs. Donald C. Daum
Mr. & Mrs. Michael Davenport
Mr. & Mrs. Joseph Daverman
Dortha Davey
John R. Davidson
Ruth D. Davidson
Mrs. Elizabeth Davidson-Hunt
Bill & Maureen Davies
Mr. & Mrs. Jeffrey R. Davies
Lloyd A. Davies
Mr. & Mrs. Alan Davis
Anne Davis
Barbara J. Davis
Carl E. Davis
Mr. & Mrs. Lee A. Davis
Mr. & Mrs. John L. Davis Jr.
Miss Mary H. Davis
Randy & Wendy Davis
Mr. & Mrs. Roland Davis
Roy A. Davis, M.D.
Walter & Edwina Davis
Mildred E. Davisson
Helen Dawkins
Mrs. Mildred Day
Ralph W. Day, M.D.
Doris De Boer
Nancy J. De Boer
Mr. & Mrs. Warren De Jong
Ron De Vries
Margaret E. DeGlopper
Mr. & Mrs. Roger A. DeHaan
Willem & Amy DeHoogh
Rev. & Mrs. Daniel D. DeJesus
Miss Isabel DeJesus
John & Carla DeLancy
Mr. & Mrs. Mark DeMoss
Mr. & Mrs. Dennis DeRight
George & Barb Deakin
Beth A. Deck
Mrs. Martin Decker
Robert & Corrie Decker
Mr. & Mrs. James Deffenbaugh
John & Joan Delk
B. J. Dellinger
Dr. & Mrs. J. G. Den Hartog
Rev. Bert Den Herder
John & Pauline Denhart
Mr. & Mrs. Walter Dennhardt
Madeline K. Dennis

Sue Dennis
Connie Jean Dettmer
David H. Detzer
Glenn & Nancy Devlin
Joseph DiPietro
Mr. & Mrs. Stanley J. Dick
Gordon & Myra E. Dickerson
Carl & Joyce Dieda
Rosemary M. Diehl
Rutherford O. Diehl
Mrs. Alice M. Dielschneider
Dr. & Mrs. G. A. Dierdorff
Len & Shirley Dietz
Bob & Ruth Dillon
Thomas Herb Dimmock
Mr. & Mrs. Samuel J. Dimon
Karen Disarufino
Dorothy M. Divers
Mr. & Mrs. Brendan Dixon
Howard C. Doane
Mr. & Mrs. Don Dobbins
Peggy S. Dobbins
Mr. & Mrs. Hilmer G. Dobler
Mr. & Mrs. Stanley Dockstader
Daryle & Brenda Doden
Mr. Richard E. Dodson
Hulda Doerksen
Peg Dolan
Mrs. E. R. Doll
Charles G. Domina Jr.
Michael & Rebecca Dornoff
Jane W. Dorsey
Mr. & Mrs. Chris Dover
Walter & Theolyn Dowdle
David Downe
Lisa & Michael Downey
Bruce Downing
Mr. & Mrs. James R. Downing
Mr. Keith S. Doyle
Eliner Drake
Kyle & Jaye Drake
Thomas Drennon
Mr. & Mrs. John Dressler
Lt. Col. & Mrs. Warren S. Dronen
Laura M. Drown
Mr. & Mrs. Daniel J. Drummond
Peter & Mary Drury
Mr. & Mrs. Huei Chi-Chung Du
Eleanor & Art Duble
Roy & Ann Dudley
Mr. & Mrs. James F. Dugan Jr.
Mr. & Mrs. Al Dumire
Ernst Dummermuth
Virgiwin R. Duncan
Debra Harrison Dunlap
Stephen & Connie Dunlap
John H. Dunn
Nancy Kay Dunn
Norman Dunsmore
G. A. Durand

Dennis & Felicia Durling
Virgil H. Durrance
D. Craig Durstewitz
David & Linda Dutton
Dr. R. N. Dutton
Ms. Phyllis Dvorak
Edith R. Dykes
Mr. & Mrs. Harry Dykstra
Doloris H. Earley
Mrs. Esther Earnest
Rev. Eloise East
Danny & Lillian Easterly
Richard Easton
Ann Eastridge
Mr. & Mrs. David H. Eaton
Bonne Ebel
Russell I. Ebel
John H. Eberhardt Jr.
Dr. & Mrs. George H. Eddy
Reginald & Loutrell Edenfield
Brian W. Edwards
Mr. & Mrs. Gary Edwards
John S. Egan
Ms. Ruth M. Egeland
Ms. Mildred M. Eicher
Keith C. Eickelberg
Mrs. Violet Eidt
Mr. & Mrs. Kenneth Einarsen
Mr. & Mrs. Robert A. Einstein
Ray Ekvall
Dee Elble
Andrew & Rosemary Elias
Mr. & Mrs. Kenneth Joel Elkins
Marilyn & Russell Ellingsworth
Ginger Leigh Elliott
Roy & Odene Elliott
Mr. & Mrs. E. W. Ellis
Frances L. Ellis
Nancy B. Ellis
Dorothy & Al Ellison
Mr. & Mrs. Herbert A. Ellison
Paula & Zula Ellison
Deke Ellwanger
Lewis Enderle
The Endicott Family
Everett D. Engebretson
Warren & Lois Engelbart
Joan & John Enger
David L. Englert
Louis A. Ensenat, M.D.
Mr. & Mrs. Willie Entz
Susan H. Epp
Mrs. Mildred Epps
Mr. & Mrs. Larry A. Erb
Al Erck
Boris & Ginny Erdiakoff
Leona Erickson
Pam Varney Erickson
William Erker
Mrs. Edna Erpestad

Cathy L. Estes
Don & Sue Estes
Betty M. Estridge
Anthony & Myrna Ettaro
E. Z. Eugene
Elnora Evans
John L. Ewert
C. Stuart Exon, M.D.
John C. Eyster Jr.
Ruth Fairrington
Thomas & Sonia Faletti
Richard & Maria C. Fanslau
Lynn B. Farrington
Mrs. Helen E. Farson
Alvin & Olga Fast
Rev. Thomas A. Federline
Mr. & Mrs. Edmund Federwitz
William & Ruby Fedro
Margery A. Fehling
Kelli Feigenbutz
Paul & Deborah Fellows
Flip & Marguerite Felton
Rev. Ronald D. Fenner
Carl F. Fenstermaker
Mr. & Mrs. James A. Ferguson
Sharon Fetters
Mrs. Joseph F. Fiato
Anne C. Fichtner
Sterling A. Fielding
Mr. & Mrs. Gerald Fikse
Steve & Donna File
Ms. Pat Finlay
V. Shirley Fish
Mrs. Anna A. Fishel
Doris R. Fisher
Jan Fisher & Tom Baker
Robert & Rachel Fisher
Dick & Lucie Flack
Lois Fladager
Alma C. Flanagan
Barbara & James Fleming
Jonathan & Karen Fleming
Mrs. Orlonzo Flanders
Venetia F. Fleming
Mr. Thomas L. Florence
Stephen W. Florschuetz
Mr. & Mrs. Leonard A. Fogleman
Mrs. Caroline Folkers
Jay & Marian Folkert
Marshall Foose
Bart Foradora
Alice L. Forbes
Mr. & Mrs. James Ford
William D. Ford
Craig & Barbara Forney
Ed & Sheila Fortier
Katharine S. Fortune
Emil M. Fossan
Dean & Nancy Foster
Stephen R. Foster

Mr. & Mrs. Dallas Foster Jr.
Emily E. Foutz
Debbie Fowler
Betty R. Fox
Mr. & Mrs. Oliver Fox
Nancy Francuz
Ms. Florence M. Franey
Mrs. Arthur S. Frank
James L. Frank
Frank & Jane Frankman
Mr. & Mrs. Gary Frantz
Mr. & Mrs. Irvin Franzen
Col. & Mrs. James F. Fraser
Betty M. Fratarcangelo
Mrs. Thomas W. Frazier
Mrs. Donald Fream
Mr. & Mrs. Michael T. Freda
George Frederick Jr.
Mr. Grover Frederick
Vernon W. Frederickson
Martha Free
Elsie W. Freeman
Mr. & Mrs. James R. Freeman
Mr. & Mrs. Woodrow W. French
Harold E. Frey
Lois Frey
Mr. & Mrs. Robert G. Frey
Rachel Frick
Robert W. Frieling
Claudia Wehdeking Friend
Mrs. Doris Friggle
Mr. & Mrs. Thomas Frinell
Mr. & Mrs. Robert C. Fringer
Mark P. Fritz
Mrs. Shirley Fritz
Leslie C. Fritzlan
George & Mildred Froehlich
Richard L. Froehlich
Mr. & Mrs. Felix A. Froese
Sam Frontiera
Mrs. James W. Frost
Bud & Jan Frye
Mr. & Mrs. William L. Fudge
David & Kim Fuhrmann
Karen A. Fuller
Mr. & Mrs. Robert J. Fuller
Mr. & Mrs. John R. Fulton
Anne V. Furno
Mrs. E. Priscilla Fyffe
Mr. & Mrs. Arden Gackenbach
Mr. Matthew Gadson
Tom & Bobbie Gaffigan
Eleanor Nave Gagg
Mr. & Mrs. Charles W. Gallutia
Mrs. Ruth H. Galyean
Virginia Gann
Arthur Gannon
Frances Gardner
Mr. & Mrs. Herbert A. Gardner Jr.
Pauline Garman

Mrs. David Garnett
Bob & Marion Garthwait
Martin M. Gaudiose
Rev. Arthur G. Gauerke
Mrs. Amos Gaume
Ms. Amanda Gaumer
Ted Gaze
Mr. & Mrs. George W. Gebhardt
Peter & Chris Geddes
Mr. & Mrs. Roland Geib
Warren O. Geib
Arlene Geibe
Mr. & Mrs. Robert A. Gemmill
LeoNora Pearson Gent
Rodney Gentil
Stephen H. George
Claudia Gerdes
Mrs. Hilding C. Gerdlund
Mrs. Mimi Germer
Rev. & Mrs. Herman D. Gerrish
Fred J. Gertler
Karl A. Gettmann
Mr. & Mrs. Kenneth L. Gibble
C. Leon Gibbs
Mary T. Gibson
Peggy S. Gibson
Doris L. Giffin
David Gilbert
John Gilbert
Wanda G. Gilchrist
Melvia Giles
Bob & Linda Gill
James R. Gill
Mr. & Mrs. George J. Gillen Jr.
Dr. & Mrs. James P. Gills
Richard & Leila Gilman
Brian Gilpin
Leon & Millie Girdner
Al Gittens
John C. Glance
Newton J. Gleason
Stewart Glenn
God's Love Ministries
Dr. & Mrs. Earl R. Godwin
Sherry Goetz
Dr. Felix Goizueta
Mr. & Mrs. C. Spencer Goldsborough
Bernard & Gwen Gonyaw
Donna D. Good
Georgia Anne Good
Jim & Dorcas Good
Jay & Jennie Goodman
Elizabeth Goodrich
Heather Goodwin
Pastor & Mrs. A. Culver Gordon
Mrs. Mary Gordon
Tom Gordy
Phyllis Gorea-Vannatta
Mr. & Mrs. Charley Gortsema
Mr. & Mrs. F. Laurence Gosnell

Ellen E. Goss
Jann Gouge
Marguerite Gould
Mike & Heather Gowan
Marion Goward
Ms. Marie Grabowski
Mr. & Mrs. Willis R. Grafe
Henry J. Graham Jr.
Mr. & Mrs. Les Graham
Mildred L. Graham
Ciro P. Granatini
Mr. & Mrs. Louis J. Grande
Irving & Ruth Granderson
Kenneth W. Grant
Mert Grant
Thelma L. Grant
Worth & Kathryn Grant
Mark & Lelar Gravatt
Mr. & Mrs. Harold Graves
Ouida Gray
Mr. Thomas E. Gray
Anna J. Graybill
Mrs. Grady Green
Dr. & Mrs. Scott Green
Arline E. Greenlee
Dr. & Mrs. J. Harold Greenlee
Harold H. Greenwald
Mr. & Mrs. Dale Greer
Mr. & Mrs. Joseph Grefenstette
Alonzo E. Gregg
Grady M. Gregory
Susan D. Gregory
James W. Greig
Julian Gresham
Charlotte Gribauskas
Melvin R. Grieser
Harry & Eva Griffin
Leslie Griffin-Andrews
Rev. & Mrs. Richard H. Griffith
Mr. & Mrs. Barton K. Grigg
Erskine R. Grimes
Karen & Bill Griswold
John & Marian Groff
Mr. Martin Groff
John D. Grollimund
Sherry D. Grosse
Mr. & Mrs. Loren C. Grossi
Joseph H. Grostephan
Mrs. Katie M. Grounds
Dr. Vernon & Ann Grounds
Mr. & Mrs. Raul Guerrero
Ray Guinsbeck
Ida U. Gulbro
Dr. & Mrs. Terry Gundlach
Mrs. Earl A. Gunning
Mr. & Mrs. Jim Gunther
Phyllis J. Gunther
Ms. June Gustafson
Ms. Neva Gustafson
Victor H. Gustafson

Mr. Joseph L. Guthrie Sr.
Hector Gutierrez
Bill & Susan Haagsma
Mrs. B. J. Haan
Edith Hadley
Gordon Hadley
Mrs. Betty C. Haesloop
Jay L. Hagerich
Mabel E. Hagey
Mr. & Mrs. Alvin J. Hahn
Theodore Haibeck
Paul L. Haig
Mr. & Mrs. K. R. Haines
Mr. & Mrs. Eric E. Halbach
J. Douglas Haley
Minnie Haley
Cuba H. Hall
Dennis D. Hall
Mr. & Mrs. Harwood L. Hall
Mr. & Mrs. John E. Hall Jr.
Mrs. Ruth Hall
Audra M. Hamaker
T. C. & Anna Hamaker
Wallace E. Hamburg
Donald & Charlotte Hamilton
Mrs. Ernest Hamilton
Leasteen H. Hamilton
Ronald T. Hamilton, D.M.D.
Suzanne & Bob Hamilton
Reverend Thomas Hamilton
Mr. & Mrs. T. J. Hammel
Bob & Margie Hammer
Mrs. Linda J. (Clark) Hammond
Renee Hammond
Mr. & Mrs. William M. Hammond
Ronald & Rebecca Hamner
Mrs. Roberta S. Hampton
Larry & Grace Hamrick
Jack D. Hancox
Horace B. Hand
Nancy Handwerk
Ted & Iris Hanes
Ken Hangliter
A. Burton Hankins
Crystal A. E. Hannigan
Tuulikki Hanninen
John D. Hannum
Alpha G. Hansen
Mrs. Jemima Hansen
Bob & Flo Hanson
Mrs. Charles Hanson
Mr. & Mrs. John K. Hanson
Lucille E. Hanson
Milo C. Hanson
Mr. & Mrs. Thomas D. Harbaugh
Mr. & Mrs. Arthur Harbeck
Bruce Harbison
Dianne Harbison
Mr. & Mrs. Orlando B. Harder
Virginia R. Hardin

Joanna D. Harding
William F. Harelson
Dick & Lois Harlow
Mr. & Mrs. William J. Harmon
Mr. & Mrs. Menno Harms
Naji Haroun
Linda C. Harper
Mike & Connie Harper
Vashti B. Harper
Edward D. Harrell
Robert C. Harris
Vernon C. Harris
Dr. & Mrs. Clifford Harrison
Norman B. Harrison
Mr. & Mrs. Gregory Hart
Lu Ella J. Hart
John Hartford
Mr. & Mrs. Darwin Hartman
Larry & Ruth Hartman
Marguerite V. Hartman
Mary Carolyn Hartman
Harriet E. Hartquist
Dolores R. Hartsell
Levi & Irene Hartzler
D. C. & Sadie Harwood
Mr. Richard Haseley
Pastor & Mrs. Eugene Hasselquist
Everett & Barbara Hassing
Mr. & Mrs. Robin L. Hasting
George & Virginia Hastings
Daniel & Kari Hatch
Mildred Hatchett
Joan Toller Hatfield
Fern Hathaway
Mr. & Mrs. James L. Hausman II
Madeline Haveman
Howard & Dorothy Havens
Ms. Eleanor C. Havis
LeRoy & Anna Mae Hawthorne
Dr. Jack & Anna Hayford
Mr. & Mrs. Don H. Hayne
Mr. Jean F. Haynes
Mr. & Mrs. Clemeth F. Head
Dora M. Head
Christine C. Healy
William M. Hearn
Robert E. Heath
Mrs. Elma M. Heaton
Mr. & Mrs. Ernest P. Hebert Jr.
Hazel M. Heck
Mr. & Mrs. Larry Hedgepeth
Bill H. Heerlein
Hans & Myrtle Heia
Dorothy Heidlebaugh
Linda L. Heikkinen
Elizabeth R. Heil
Charles E. Heinlen
Mrs. Wandah Purdy Helgeson
Thomas A. Helinski
Alois U. Hellstern

Mrs. Betty Helmer
Carol R. Helmholz
Norris L. Helstrom
Mr. & Mrs. David F. Henderson
Irene S. Henderson
Mr. & Mrs. Gordon L. Hendricks
Mr. & Mrs. James R. Hendrix Jr.
Patricia J. Hendzel
Gail B. Henjum
Fredrick & Vanessa Henley
Mrs. Raymond H. Henning
Robert C. Henning
Shawn & Sara Henning
Carl & Kathryn Hensley
Mrs. Virginia L. Henson
Ms. Brenda Herdon
John Hermistone
Michael & Laura Hernandez
Sergio & Maria Hernandez
Mrs. Lola Herndon
Edwin & Judith Herr
Mr. & Mrs. Don W. Herron
Camilla C. Hersh, M.D.
John K. & Reba Hershey
Ronald Hesche
Esther Hess
Helen M. Hess
Dr. & Mrs. R. B. Hess
Mr. & Mrs. J. Heston
Lydia Hewitt
Shirley M. Hewett
Oscar & Georgie Heyman
Brad Hibbs
Nora J. Hickam
Mrs. Marion H. Hickerson
Laura B. Hicks
Dr. & Mrs. Tom Hicks
Kevin Highfield
Cam & Lynwood Hightower
Father Hilkert
Gary L. Hill Sr.
Norma J. Hinderlie
Mr. & Mrs. David B. Hinshaw
Connie Hipple
Peggy K. Hirai
Karen Mosher Hite
Cynthia K. Hobart
Lola L. Hobbs
Mr. & Mrs. Ivan Hochstetler
Mrs. Marian J. Hodges
Dr. Kathleen A. Hodgman
Susan Paulo Hoecker
Charles Hoffer
Mr. Berlie Hoffstot
Mr. & Mrs. Hampton W.
   Hoge Jr.
Elizabeth S. Hogg
Robert & Phyllis Hohnholz
Takuo Hohri
Scot & Jaclyn Hoiland

Lu Hoin
Robert Ford Holland
Chuck & Evonne Holloway
Ron Holloway
Don & Jann Holm
Heidi Holm
Inga Holm
Reuben & Margaret Holm
Mr. & Mrs. Arthur Holman
Mrs. Kathryn J. Holmes
Paul G. Holsted
Lois S. Honsberger
Doug A. Hood
Mike & Amy Hood
Mr. & Mrs. Wm. D. Hood
Ken & Lucile Hooker
Charlotte L. Hoover
Mr. Elton L. Hopkins
Mr. & Mrs. Gary J. Hopkins
Floyd Horany
Novelyn Horton
Lynn & Donna Hoselton
Lu Ann Hostetter
Mr. & Mrs. August L. Hoting
Russell & Audrey Houghton
Ed & Nancy Houle
Col. Kenneth House
Tom & Judy House
Bg. & Mrs. Houston P. Houser III
Michael M. How
Mrs. Anna Lou Howard
Annie W. Howard
Lena L. Howard
Calvin & Lois Howe
J. Elisabeth Howell
Martha Jean Howell
Thelma L. Howell
William C. Howell Jr.
Dr. & Mrs. Chen C. Hsu
Kent L. Hubbard
Stephen & Christine Hubbard
Christine Hubert
Lark Hudik
Rosemarie Hudson
Tom Hudson
Donald W. Huffman
Martha E. Hughell
Alfred Hughes
Florence E. Hughes
Rebecca C. Hughes
Mr. & Mrs. John M. Hugnet
Doris M. Hugunin
Mrs. John T. Hultgren
David Hume
Shelley C. Hume
Janis L. Humphrey
R. A. Humphrey
Mr. & Mrs. Burnett Hunt
Charles J. Hunter
Marcia J. Hunter

Mrs. Wesley R. Hurst
Pauline Husher
Ted & Glenna Huskey
Fred Huston
Rev. & Mrs. Clarence Hutchens
David J. Hutchinson
Frank Hutton
Rev. & Mrs. Elee Hyden
Susan D. Hylton
Miss Donna M. Ianacone
Dr. Dwain C. Illman
Dave & Judi Imperato
Nancy Crockett Ince
Industrial Air Products Inc.
Mr. & Mrs. Dean M. Ingraham
John & Janet Innes
Stuart C. Irby Jr.
Reverend Joan L. Irminger
Virginia L. Irvine
Dr. & Mrs. Richard Ivance
Jean Marie Ivery
John Izenbaard
Orville E. Jack
Charles E. Jackson
Mr. Anthony Jacob
Timothy J. Jacobs
Mrs. Aldora Jacobsen
John W. Jacobson
Jim & Judy Jacobson
Monte & Diane Jahnke
J. Douglas James
Mr. Lee A. James
Lucille A. James
Paul S. James
Sandra James
Mary R. Jamison
Wayne & Ann Jamison
Dr. & Mrs. Paul W. Jamisons
Mr. & Mrs. Steve Jankord
Mrs. Marion C. Janney
Carol & Nick Jansen
Ken & Janet Janzen
Stan Jarrett
Dr. & Mrs. J. Gregory Javornisky
Gaines Ray Jeffcoat
Elizabeth & Robert Jeffe
Mr. & Mrs. Marlin E. Jeffers
Mr. & Mrs. Hugh M. Jefferson
Sherylyn Jeffries
Miss Dianne Jenkins
John & Virginia Jenkins
Ms. Grace Jennings
Barbara & Wayland Jensen
Genevieve Jensen
Mr. Harold J. Jensen
Vicki L. Jensen
Ruth Jepson
Susan M. Jesser
Dorothy A. Jevitt, R.N.
Mr. & Mrs. Dave Jewell

Mrs. William R. Jewis
Ethelyn L. Jimerfield
Clara C. Jobe
Sharon Johannsen
Mr. & Mrs. A. Kenneth Johnson
Allan Johnson
Arlene L. Johnson
Mr. & Mrs. B. R. Johnson
Mr. & Mrs. Bert Johnson
Mrs. Betty Johnson
Betty V. Johnson
Bill & Ruth Johnson
Brad & Karol Johnson
Carolyn Johnson
Dan Johnson
Dave & Lynne Johnson
Diane Johnson
Elvira J. Johnson
Emogene Johnson
Mr. & Mrs. Eric C. Johnson
Gilbert & Eileen Johnson
Gladys C. Johnson
Greta E. Johnson
Helen C. Johnson
Mr. & Mrs. James W. Johnson
Janet Johnson
Mr. & Mrs. John A. Johnson Jr.
Judith C. Johnson
Larry & Beth Johnson
Oscar & Elaine Johnson
Pauline M. Johnson
Peter & Christy Johnson
Phil & Alice Johnson
Ray & Carol Johnson
Robin Johnson
Russ & Lois Johnson
Mrs. Ruth Johnson
Terrance G. Johnson
Thad P. Johnson
Virginia A. Johnson
Vivian M. Johnson
Wm. C. Johnson Jr.
Barb & Dave Johnston
David H. Johnston, M.D.
Mr. & Mrs. Howard L. Johnston
Thomas & Donna Johnston
Bert & Diane Jones
Dan M. Jones
James T. Jones
Jan Jones
Mrs. Lucile D. Jones
Marie P. Jones
Mrs. Myrtle T. Jones
Mrs. Robert F. Jones
Miss Roberta E. Jones
Wanda E. Jones
William Converse Jones
Betty L. Jordan
Edward & Alice Jordan
Mrs. Margaret Jordan

Mr. & Mrs. O. W. Josserand
Ms. Kathleen M. Joyce
Wayne & Elnora Joyce
M. C. Joynt
Dorothy Judy
Robin Julian
Mr. & Mrs. Dwight A. Jurey
Rev. & Mrs. Robert Kahly
Mr. & Mrs. Richard O. Kaley
Celia A. Kallas
Karen Staymates Kallenborn
Anne & Doug Kallesen
Rev. & Mrs. Charles Kamp
Ina Kannasto
Ruth E. Kantner
Kathleen D. Kantrud
Gerald Benord Karfs
Diane Eaves Karim
Elli Karjalainen
Gary Karnig
Jan Kary
Sue Kasting
David Katka
Edward I. Kats
Harold J. Kats
Mr. & Mrs. Allen L. Kauffman
Mr. & Mrs. Monroe Kauffman
Tom & Dona Kauth
Mr. & Mrs. Jake Kawakami
Mr. & Mrs. William C. Kayser
Dr. & Mrs. Russell B. Keating
Lori L. Keck
Mr. & Mrs. Vaderon Keeney
George & Irene Kefalas
M. E. Keith
William Joseph Keith
Mr. & Mrs. N. A. Keithley Jr.
Mr. & Mrs. Kelly Keithly
Howard & Cynthia Kelenbenz
Grace M. Kellaway
Connie Kellermyer
Nelson Kelley
Mr. & Mrs. Thomas Kelsey
June Kemalyan
Richard L. Kemp
Mr. & Mrs. Gary Kendall
David S. Kendig
Mrs. Jane E. Kengeter
Ella Mae Kennedy
Mr. & Mrs. Robert Kennedy
Ruth P. Kentzel
Mary Dee Keown
Mrs. Shirley Kernodle
Pamela G. Kerr
Karen Kerrigan
Art & Martha Keshian
Marian Kessell
Mr. & Mrs. Edwin Kessler
Harold & Wilma Key
Russell & Naomi Kice

Mr. & Mrs. Hubert V. Kiehl
Dr. Frank N. Kik
Mrs. Curt Killinger
Mr. & Mrs. Vernon L. Kimpel
Lloyd & Elsie Kina
Mr. & Mrs. John C. Kiner
Arlene A. King
Dr. Charles C. King
Mr. & Mrs. David A. King
Frank C. King
M. Alberta Skinner King
Mrs. Pauline T. King
Peggy King
Virginia King
Nason E. Kinkaid
Miss Christy M. Kinnerson
Dr. & Mrs. Robert B. Kinney
Mr. & Mrs. John M. Kirby
Mr. & Mrs. Robert M. Kirchner
Richard C. Kirk
Rob & Louise Kirkpatrick
Mr. & Mrs. T. W. Kirkpatrick
Dr. & Mrs. Glen A. Kirsch
Mrs. Barbara Kisley
Chris Kitterman
Vernon & Grace Klaassen & Family
Leonard & Rosalie Klassen
Dale & Karen Klingberg
Mr. & Mrs. Gerrit J. Klinge
Mr. & Mrs. Raymond Kliphardt
Carolyn M. Knecht
Leah D. Kneebone
John & Nancy Knol
Frank & Sandy Knoll
Dr. & Mrs. Walter Knouse
Nate & Nadine Knowles
Ethel June Williams Knox
Mr. & Mrs. James Knox
Russell D. Knudsen
Maynard "Knute" Knutson
James A. Kobus
Geraldine M. Koenig
Harlan & Esther Koenig
Lou Kohlman
Mr. & Mrs. Robert E. Kohoutek
Tom & Debbie Kolarik
Aaron & Eunice Kolb
Tim & Lyn Kool
Nelson & Sue Kopatz
Kopis Family
Korean United Church of Phila.
Vicki Kost
Jean W. Kouba
Ms. Chris Kowalonek
Alice L. Kraemer
Lyle V. Kragh
Jane Kraitzer
Miss Ruth A. Kramer
Mr. & Mrs. Timothy J. Kranick
Harry & Pearl Krause

Mr. & Mrs. Orley W. Kreger
Mrs. Dana D. Kreider
Robert & Ve Kreke
Mr. & Mrs. Richard E. Krell
Bradley & Patricia Kremensek
Wayne & Sharon Krestel
Margaret Krolikowski
James L. Kroon
David L. Krueger Sr.
Patricia Ellison Kruse
Stephen & Karen Krusich
Mr. & Mrs. Paul Kuck
Wallace & Marian Kuck
Mr. & Mrs. Thomas Kuenning
Mr. & Mrs. William Kuhlman
Marie Kuiper
Betty J. Kulla
Orville & Vera Kurtz
Mr. & Mrs. Thomas Kurtz
Shirley & Leiv Kvamme
Mr. & Mrs. Vincent Kyriak
Diane C. LaVallie
Michael S. Labos
Ginny Lagers
Mrs. Jeanne C. Lagervall
Vieno & Edwin Lahti
Ruth B. Laird
Mrs. Daniel Lam
Ava Beard Lamar
Frank Lammers Jr.
H. Jerome Lancaster
Ollie Mae Landen
Leila & Don Landgrebe
Mrs. Violet Laney
Gertrude G. Langford
Bill & Roberta Langland
Marilyn Lanier
Robin & Allen Lankford
Mr. & Mrs. Tom Lano
Mrs. David D. Lardin
Mr. & Mrs. D. Burton Larkey
Dorothy M. Larsen
Esther E. Larson
Mr. & Mrs. Frederick Larson
Gladys S. Larson
Harold & Verna Larson
LouAnn Larson
Virginia Lee Larson
Wallace & Margaret Larson
Mr. & Mrs. William J. Larson
Scott J. Lash
Mr. & Mrs. Terry D. Lashley
Richard Hill Lauber
Mr. & Mrs. Charles H. Lauck Jr.
Carol J. Laude
Loretta Laugere
William Henry Lawrence III
William & Patsy Laycoax
Donald L. LeBlanc
F. Inez Lear

Mrs. Connie Dear Lee
Donald S. Lee
Mrs. Frankie M. Lee
Mrs. Marion Lee
Woo Jin Lee
William T. Leeds
Ruby A. Leedy
John C. Lehl
Dr. & Mrs. David A. Lehman
J. Wilmer & Gladys Lehman
John P. Lehman, D.D.S.
Mr. & Mrs. Phillips D. Lehman
Leona H. Lehner
Danny & Carol Leichty
Lois J. Leidig
Lori Leining
Werner & Sandra Lemke
Mr. & Mrs. J. Louis Lempesis
Dennis & Deanna Lenz
Mr. & Mrs. Larry F. Leonard
John Leonardson
Mr. & Mrs. Harold C. Leslie
Mrs. Sandra J. Lessard
Mr. & Mrs. Les M. Lester
Elizabeth Lettau
Gary L. Leu
Jarett Todd Levitsky
Walter J. Lewicki
C. Gordon Lewis
Mr. & Mrs. Edgar S. Lewis
Mr. & Mrs. Floyd W. Lewis
Mr. & Mrs. Robert S. Lewis
Margaret Lickfold
Scott Liechty
Rev. & Mrs. David Liefeld
Joan W. Lin
David H. Lincoln
Mrs. Louise Lincoln
Mr. & Mrs. John Lindeman
Doug & Lynn Lindle
Mr. & Mrs. Harry Lindner
Jane E. Lindstrom
Ruby Winslow Linn
LaVerna Lipp
Mrs. Dot M. Lis
John & Blanche Litle
Brian, Cyndi, Marci & Ben Litwiller
Ralph & Marge Lloyd
Marianne K. Locke
Mrs. Betty Lockee
Jeff Locker
Mr. Millard P. Lockley
Mr. & Mrs. Richard Loescher
Louise Loewen
Bill Lohrenz
Mr. & Mrs. John J. Lokker
Phil & Sarah Lomax
Mr. & Mrs. Richard A. Long
Robert Alton Long
Virginia B. Long

Helen, Larry & Laurie Longshore
Mr. & Mrs. Harold A. Loomis
Andres Lopez
Mrs. Maria A. Lopez
Ms. Dolores Lorenzo
Rachel Lotter
Patricia Love
Marjorie A. Lovrak
Mary Carolyn Lovvorn
Mr. & Mrs. Harold C. Lowe
Mrs. Lucille Lowenberg
JoAnne Lucas
Mr. Elmer Luckritz
Karen L. Ludwig
Mr. & Mrs. Art Luedeke
Norman & Virginia Luepschen
Miss Lucile Lukens
Richard Lundgren
Mr. Edward Luongo
Mr. & Mrs. Fred D. Luper
Donald Lutton, D.V.M.
Dave Lyke
Willie Lyles
Helen T. Lyman
Gary Alan Lynema
John & Doris Lynn
Deford L. Lyons
James W. Lyons
Clifford P. Lytle
Emily G. Lytle
Mr. & Mrs. Vance E. Lytle
Amy M. Mac Lean
Al MacDonald
Elaine K. MacLeod
Mr. & Mrs. James R. Mackay
Mr. & Mrs. Dale E. Madison
Dr. Jim & Linda Magnusen
Helen L. Magnuson
M. Betty Magnuson
Esther Magnussen
Manly & Mary Magsig
Mr. & Mrs. Gene L. Mahn
Mr. & Mrs. Joseph Mahon
Kenneth & Helen Mahood
Mr. & Mrs. Hans Maier
Linda Malchow
Ana M. Maldonado
Nelson & Florence Malkus
Edward & Helen Malwitz
Mr. Lee V. Manatis
Peter & Kathryn Mandarino
Mr. & Mrs. James Mander
Frances B. Manville
Grant & Viola March
Mr. & Mrs. Jim Marcy
Sam Mardian III
Carl J. Mari
Sherri Marinus
Barbara Markus
Kenneth S. Marmaras

Mr. Angel Marquez
Mr. & Mrs. W. D. Marrs
Elaine Mars
Dr. & Mrs. H. H. Marsh
Mr. & Mrs. Vincent A. Martens
Aliene Richey Martin
Mrs. Beatrice D. Martin
Mr. & Mrs. Dallas S. Martin
Herb & Joyce Martin
James & Janet Martin
Joe & Marge Martin
L. Howard Martin
Mr. & Mrs. Larry Martin
Rev. Mary E. Martin
Michael & Sandra Martin
Paul Martin
Dr. & Mrs. R. Russell Martin
Rachel W. Martin
Mr. & Mrs. Stanley L. Martin
Mr. & Mrs. William K. Martin
Virginia M. Marullo
Mrs. Evelyn T. Maschek
L. C. Massey
Ernest S. Mast
Wayne & Betty Mast
Mr. & Mrs. Thomas D. Masten
Elna Maston
Melanie H. Materson
Mr. & Mrs. Raymond H. Mathisen
Belle Mathys
Karine Matter
James P. Mattern
Mr. & Mrs. James M. Mattheis
Mr. & Mrs. Richard C. Matthews
Mr. & Mrs. Harry L. Mattimore
Mrs. Loretta Mattison
Henry & Fran Mauldin
Mildred B. Maurer
Mrs. Rhoda Maust
Rev. Chris May
Allan & Lois Mayer
Eloise E. Mayfield
Mr. & Mrs. D. Mayoros
Mr. & Mrs. Sidney F. McAllister
Hoover McBee
Mrs. Marion McBride
John T. McBryde
Sharon G. McCall
Mr. & Mrs. Luke McCarley
A. K. & Sue McCarley Jr.
Daina L. McCarthy
Mr. & Mrs. Stanley G. McCarty
Linda McCauley
Sam & Vera McCleery
Mary M. McClelland
Mrs. Margaret McClure
Mr. & Mrs. Ken McClurkin
Olive D. McClymont
Mrs. Eleanor S. McCollum
Mr. & Mrs. F. N. McCorkle III

Ralph E. McCormick
Mr. & Mrs. Scott McCormick
Rogers M. McCrae
Mr. & Mrs. H. D. McCraw
Mrs. Renee McCullah
Iro A. McCulloch
Mary J. McCune
Janet L. McCutchen
Rev. & Mrs. Gilbert K. McDonald
James C. McDonald
Rev. Rex McDonald
Pastor & Mrs. Timothy McDonald
Eloise McDougal
Russell T. McDougal
Opal E. McEachern
Mrs. Mae H. McElhinney
Mrs. Willard L. McEwen
Kent C. McGahey
Eileen McGarvey
Patricia McGhee
Henry McGrew
Jan McIntosh
Hubert & Vera McIntyre
Fran & Joe McKay
Ries & Carol McKee
Mary E. McKeever
Mr. & Mrs. Sturgis McKeever
Berta McKenzie
Stanley C. McKenzie
Robert M. McKnight
Ms. Dorothea J. McLaughlin
Mr. & Mrs. Thomas McLaughlin
John McLean
Mr. & Mrs. Joseph C. McLeland
Elizabeth McManus
Mrs. J. Claire McMartin
Paul B. McMorris
Joan H. McNeely
Mr. & Mrs. Jeffery C. McNeice
Mr. & Mrs. J. D. McNeil
Mrs. Velma McNitt
Betty McNutt
Walter J. McPherson
Mr. & Mrs. Harrison E. McVay Sr.
John McWilliams
Dennis & Cindy Means
Philip Lawrence Meddleton
J. Frederick Medford
Ray Medich
Michael R. Meekhof
Marie E. Meenen
Ms. Denise J. Mellerup
Mr. & Mrs. Mark S. Melton
Rich & Marybeth Mendez
David J. Menkhaus
Gregg & Dee Menning
Mr. George S. Merchant
Shirley M. Mercurio
Helen G. Meredith
James E. Merlin

JANE M. METZGER
RON & LOIS MEULENBERG
DEL & LOIS MEYER
DONALD A. J. MEYER
MR. & MRS. DONALD & MELBA MEYER
HELEN D. MEYER
MS. VIOLET E. MEYER
WILLIAM & MARY MEYER
JACQUELINE S. MEYERS
BARBARA MICHALAK
S. MICHALOWSKI
MR. & MRS. DON MICHEALSEN
BILL MIDDLEBROOKS
GENE & CAROLE MIDDLETON
GEORGE MIGUELEZ
CHALMER MIKLE
MR. & MRS. JOHN D. MILHOUS
EVERT C. MILLARD
ANDY & MILLIE MILLER
MR. & MRS. BRUCE A. MILLER
CHARLES & PEGGY MILLER
CHERYL MILLER
DEAN & FREDA MILLER
DOROTHY N. MILLER
MR. & MRS. GENE MILLER
MRS. GRACE K. MILLER
REV. HAROLD & BARBARA MILLER
JENNI MILLER
KATHRINE CLEWIS MILLER
KEN & PATRICIA MILLER
DR. LIZ MILLER
MR. & MRS. LUTCHER S. MILLER
MARY MILLER
NOAH & ALTA MILLER
MRS. PEARL MILLER
RAMONA M. MILLER
MR. & MRS. THOMAS L. MILLER
MR. & MRS. WENDELL MILLER
ALICE MILLOFF
BRIAN MILLS
CAROL E. MILLS
MR. & MRS. ROBERT MILLS
MURIEL J. MILLSPAUGH
CATHARINE MINEAR
MRS. PAUL R. MINICH
CARROLL C. MISENER
JAMES & JOANNE MISGEN
MR. & MRS. JAMES MISHLER
MR. & MRS. G. KEITH MITCHELL JR.
JOHN & LINDA MITCHELL
MR. & MRS. KENNETH W. MITCHELL
STEVAN HAGOOD MIXSON
MICHAEL & WILMA MOBLEY
HAROLD W. MOELLER
M. MOKRY
MR. & MRS. STAN R. MOLER
PATSY P. MONHOLLON
ENID S. MONK
EVA M. MONSEN
WILEY & CHARLOTTE MONTGOMERY

PHIL & ALMA MOODY
MR. & MRS. B. F. MOOMAW JR.
MR. & MRS. C. DUANE MOONEY
GEORGE & MYRA MOOR
DONALD MOORE
EDITH D. MOORE
MR. JACK MOORE
JOE & MILLE MOORE
PAUL & FRAN MORABITH
MR. & MRS. JAMES N. MORGAN
MRS. LOIS F. MORGAN
MARGARET B. MORGAN
MRS. MARY J. MORGAN
MRS. CARMEL MORRIS
CLEONA H. MORRIS
CYNDY MORRIS
MRS. J. MICKEY MORRIS
DR. & MRS. ALVIN J. MOSER
KENDAL & RUBY MOSER
MS. CAROLYN MOSES
CALVIN W. MOSHER
JIM & DOT MOSS
MR. & MRS. WILLIAM T. MOSS
MRS. PAULA MOULTON
DOROTHY J. MOUNT
ELSA L. MOY
KEITH MOYDELL
EDNA W. MOYER
MR. & MRS. PRESTON E. MOYERS
MR. & MRS. EDWARD A. MUCK
RUTH C. MUIR
PAUL E. MULKEY
MICHAEL MULLANY
JEANNE MULLER
DR. & MRS DAVID MURDOCH
MR. & MRS. DAN F. MURDOCK
JACK A. MURNAHAN
MRS. FRANCES H. MURPHY
MS. JEAN MURPHY
JOAN MURPHY
ROBERT A. MURPHY
TIMOTHY P. MURPHY
DR. & MRS. STEPHEN P. MURRAY
WILLIAM A. MURRAY
LARRY AULDEN MUSGROVE
MRS. BERTHA B. MYERS
DAVID & MARY MYERS
MR. STANLEY MYERS
VIRGINIA A. MYERS
DOROTHY D. MYERSCOUGH
MARYOLIVE W. MYGATT
DAVID NAFFZIGER
RICHARD J. NAGEL JR.
ROBERT NAGEL
JOHN R. NAISBY JR.
BILLY W. NANTZ
ROBERT T. NASH
INDAR NATHASINGH
REBA & DANIEL NAUMAN
LISA NAXERA

CHRIS A. NEAL
HELEN NEDERHOED
ANDREW NEITA
MR. & MRS. CHRIS NELSON
DR. DONN & SUSAN NELSON
HEATHER A. NELSON
LAUREL NELSON
LISA K. NELSON
MR. & MRS. PATRICK NELSON
MR. & MRS. RUSSELL NELSON
L. NESBITT
DORIS NESBITT BANNISTER
RAY & SUSAN NESWOLD
MACK A. NETTLETON, PH.D.
MIKE NEVIN
MR. & MRS. RENTRO C. NEWCOMB
MR. & MRS. JACK D. NEWELL
TOM & JACKIE NEWELL
JAMES NEWMAN
MS. VERA M. NEWMAN
JENNIFER NEWNHAM
DAVID E. NEWTON
ELEANOR S. NEWTON
SHI CHUNG & SHERLYNN SUK LING NG
VINCENT NG
MARGARET T. NICHOLL
MR. & MRS. W. WAYNE NICHOLS
MARY JANE NICOLL
JOSEPH NICOLOSI JR.
RICHARD & NANCY NIEDER
CAROL D. NIELSEN
MAX NIEMANN
BARRY NILSON & LAURA LIVINGSTON
LAVERN N. NIVENS
GEORGE NIZYNSKI
NICK & TERRI NOCCIOLI
BILL & LILLIAN NOGUES
TED & JOANNE NOLLER
MR. & MRS. ROBERT J. NOLT
BOB NORBY
PAUL A. NORDGREN
DR. & MRS. WESLEY R. NORDSTROM
MR. & MRS. GLENN NORMAN
MR. & MRS. WILLIS H. NORMAN
JACKIE NORRIS
VIRGINIA M. NORRIS
SHELBY NOTTINGHAM
LARRY C. NOVAK
ELEANOR F. NOWELL
STEVEN NUGENT
MARK NUNNELEE
CARA L. NUSSBAUM
MR. & MRS. JAMES NYQUIST
RUTH EILEEN O'DELL
CHRIS & LENEE OAKLEY
TOMMY OAKS
DON L. OBE
ANNIE D. OBER
MR. & MRS. CHARLES OCHS
PETER & GAIL OCHS

REV. JEFFREY & MARGARET ODOM
DON & LAURA ODONE
MR. & MRS. WILLIAM D. OGDEN
GALE K. OGLE
BETTY P. OHLINGER
BOB & DENISE OLDACH
C. W. OLDS
MR. ARVID H. OLESON
DONALD & JOSEPHINE OLIVER
MRS. MACK OLIVER
BERNICE C. OLSEN
BETH OLSON
CINDY OLSON
MARY S. OLSON
MICHAEL H. OLSON
RALPH W. OLSON
BERTHA OMODT
ENGELUS OPPENHUIZEN
MILDRED J. ORD
PATRICIA ORR
MR. & MRS. JUAN C. ORTIZ
MR. & MRS. MELVIN F. ORTMANN
MRS. ELEANOR B. OSBORN
MS. RHEA B. OSBORNE
DONALD J. OSWALD
DEBRA OTROSINA
KEITH O. OTT
ELLEN C. OTTERBECK
MR. & MRS. JAMES F. OUIMETTE JR.
MR. & MRS. BILL J. OUTLAND
JOHN & HELEN OWENS
TOM & PATTI OWENS
MICHAEL EDWARD OZENBERGER
MR. & MRS. DAVID OZMUN
MR. & MRS. ALTON N. PACE
DR. JOHN E. PACKO
TOM PADOVANO
MISS VERNIE C. PADUL
MARK & CINDY PAGANO
MR. RONALD PAGANO-FULLER
JAMES & CANDACE PALMER
MICHAEL & MILLY PALMISANO
TONY & NITA PALONE
DOW PANNELL
MARGARET PANQUERNE
BRENDA J. PAONI
BARRY A. PAPANIA
JOSEPH H. PARABOSCHI
JIN PARK
MS. SHINAE PARK
MR. & MRS. JAY P. PARKER
MR. & MRS. JOHN A. PARKER
THOMAS G. PARRETT
DORIS & ROGER PARSELS
ANN RICE PARSONS
MS. DEBORAH PARSONS
ELIZABETH PARSONS
KENNETH L. PARSONS
ROGER PARTAIN
THOMAS & MARY ELLEN PASSINGHAM

MR. E. G. PATT
JOHN B. PATTERSON
PAUL & MARGIE PATTON
ROSALIE T. PATTON
MRS. THELMA M. PATTON
DAVID BROWNING PAUL
JOSEPH J. PAULEY
HAROLD E. PAULSON
DR. & MRS. JEFF PAXTON
KAY PAXTON
ANNA S. PEACOCK
T. A. PEACOCK
THOMAS & GINGER PEARCE
ETHEL M. PEARSON
S. GEORGE PEARSON
JAMES MILLER PECK
JOSEPH PECOTA
ESTHER PEDERSON
EVA L. PEDERSON
MISS DORIS E. R. PEEPLES
MRS. H. G. PEGRAM
GLADYS F. PEIRCE
MICHELLE A. PELKY
NAT & PEGGY PELLEGRINI
MR. & MRS. JACK PELREN
YVONNE PENDLETON
MRS. MARGUERITE PENNER
TYLER GUY PENROSE
M. JUNE PEPPER
JOYE N. PERCIVAL
GERTRUDE PERKINS
JACK & JOANN PERKINS
MR. & MRS. TOM PERKINS
LOIS PERRY
NED & CAROL PERSINGER
RICHARD A. PERSSON
JAMES M. PETER
ROBERT M. PETERHANS
JIM & THERESA PETERS
MR. & MRS. ROBERT E. PETERS
SARA PETERS
MR. & MRS. SIDNEY C. PETERS
MARGARET L. PETERSEN
DR. & MRS. VERNON J. PETERSEN
MRS. BETTY L. PETERSON
HARRY & RUTH PETERSON
JILL PETERSON
KARL F. PETERSON
P. H. PETERSON
ROBERT E. PETERSON
TIM & SHARON PETERSON
WILLARD S. PETERSON
RUTH M. PETRO
ELLEN PETTENGILL
MAURICE A. PFEIL
DON & MAUREEN PHILLIPE
ANDRENA & DONALD F. PHILLIPS
DR. ANN PHILLIPS
CINDY PHILLIPS
MRS. JOHN D. PHILLIPS

Mr. & Mrs. Kenneth H. Phillips
Lewis A. Phillips
Mr. & Mrs. Scott D. Phillips
Robert C. Phipps
William Lee Phipps
R. Kent Pickard
Marjorie Pickel
Mrs. Naome Pickhard
Roger D. Pierson
Margie Pifer
Bernice Piland
Douglas & Mary R. Piper
Ms. Florence S. Pipes
Mary F. Pitstick
David Platt
Mr. & Mrs. John F. Pletka Jr.
Mark B. Pletscher
Miriam Plitt
Suzanne Plummer
Mr. & Mrs. Robert Plunk
Mr. & Mrs. Wade E. Poet
Meta B. Poley
Charles G. Polley
Audrey J. Pollock
Ronald Polomsky
Arleene Ponton
Ed & Sandra Poock
Richard & Darlene Pool
Sharon E. Poole
Mr. & Mrs. Barry Poore
William & Louise Amanda Pope
Jacek Popiel
Gary & Arlene Popma
CH (Cpt.) Gail F. Porter
Margaret Porter
Robert F. Post Jr.
Marjorie Poston
Mrs. Bea Poteat
Mr. Mark Potter
Mrs. Ava S. Powell
Wyatt Kyle Powell
Martha B. Powers
Pat & Karen Powlen
Paula C. Pratt
Mr. & Mrs. Stephen T. Pratt
Thomas C. & Gloria Pratt
Mrs. Alice F. Preis
Roy & Gail Prescott
Rachel Pribbeno
Charles R. Price Jr.
Mrs. Helen C. Price
Janice Lee Price
Rosa Lea Price
Lola M. Pritchett
Mr. & Mrs. G. Stewart Proctor
Mr. James D. Proud
Mr. & Mrs. Ernest G. Proudfit
Mr. & Mrs. James A. Pryde
Albert G. Pryor
Mr. & Mrs. Charles T. Pu

Mr. & Mrs. H. E. Puder
Jean P. Pugh
Barbara J. Pulliam
Siri M. Pulliam
Ms. Dorothy Purse
Mrs. Alice M. Pusateri
Patricia J. Putnam
Don & Jane Ann H. Pye
Margaret J. Pyfer
James & Lois Pynch
Eleanor S. Quarles
Bob & Doris Quast
Mr. Robert Quigley
Michael & Anne Quinn
Patricia Quinn
Margaret Quirk
Gordon & Diane Quitmeyer
Mr. & Mrs. Frederic E. Rachford
Mr. Robert W. Radcliffe
Harold & Marion Radloff
Mark Raether
Mr. & Mrs. Joseph Raffa
Anthony P. Raia Jr.
Robert K. Raleigh
Irene T. Ralph
Eileen B. Ralston
Virginia Ramirez
Mr. & Mrs. Rayond M. Ramsay
Mildred Ramsey
Mrs. Everett Rand
Rev. & Mrs. Harry B.
   Randall III
Zella V. Randall
Mrs. Phyllis Ranier
Jean L. Ranquist
Dr. & Mrs. Thomas E. Rapp
William J. Rasch
Joseph & Hilda Ratcliff
Elissa Lin Rathe
Mr. & Mrs. Harold Raw
Thomas W. Ray
Mrs. Lunetta Rea
Clarence L. Reaser
Rev. & Mrs. Paul L. Reaser
Mr. Ellis E. Reber
Richard & Mary Reber
Ronald J. Rebman
Joseph Reccardi
Mr. & Mrs. A. I. Reddick
V. C. & Helen Redmon
Elnora L. Reece
Ms. Marjorie C. Reed
Maxine Reeser
Cathryne Reeves
Mr. & Mrs. Edward K. Reeves Jr.
Phil C. Reeves
Randy Regan
Mrs. Roberta Regan
Sally Rehbein
Mr. & Mrs. Glenn R. Rehnberg

Charles & Sue Reich
George C. Reid
Jim & Janette Reid
Melanie Reid
Viola C. Reid
Lela V. Reimann
Elma Reimer
Daniel D. Reinheimer
Lloyd M. Reiser
Mrs. Violet Reitz
Roger A. Rekers
Mr. & Mrs. Harry M. Rendle
Valerie Rennell
Bruce B. Rennie
Audrey E. Rennolds
Mr. & Mrs. Charles Rex
Mr. & Mrs. Dave Reynolds
Mrs. Helen T. Reynolds
Joan M. Reynolds
Mrs. Patricia A. Reynolds
Herschel A. Rhodes
Floyd E. Rice
Mr. & Mrs. James L. Rice
James A. Rickard
Deanna L. Riddle
Don & Eva Ridenour
Mr. & Mrs. H. Keith Ridgway
Rev. Nadine E. Ridgeway
Mr. & Mrs. C. J. Riedel
Doug & Margo Riedel
Eleanor Rieper
Elisabeth Rigsbee
Gerald & Helen Riley
Margie & Jerry Rilling
Mrs. Fern Ripple
Ruth N. Risch
Benjamin A. Ritz
Jorge & Taidee Rivero
Mrs. Joanne W. Roach
R. Dana Roark
Mary F. Robbins
Richard R. Robbins
Dr. & Mrs. Jon M. Robert
Mr. & Mrs. Craig Roberts
Foster & Charleen Roberts
Mrs. Jewel Faye Roberts
Linda M. Roberts
Marie Roberts
Mr. & Mrs. Maurice Roberts
Alma Robertson
Mrs. Ila W. Robertson
Mr. & Mrs. Winston M. Robinette
Captain & Mrs. David A. Robinson
Dorral P. Robinson
LeRoy J. Robinson
Markle C. Robinson
Mr. & Mrs. Michael I. Robinson
Mr. & Mrs. William E. Robinson
Dorothy M. A. Robustelli
James D. Rocco

Bill & Charlene Rodman
Ms. Lucy G. Rodman
Mary M. Rodriguez
Charles E. Roessger
Mrs. J. C. Rogers
Geraldine Rogier
Susan M. Rolls
Kenneth Roman Jr.
Marye Roman
Mr. & Mrs. John Romberger
Rev. & Mrs. Don B. Rood
Mr. & Mrs. William G. Roost
Mrs. Dorothy D. Roper
Nicole Rorrer
Janet B. Rosen
Robert R. Rosenberg
Hardy B. Ross
Robert M. Ross
Mr. & Mrs. William N. Rosser
Mr. & Mrs. James R. Rostek
Mrs. Lois I. Roth
Ms. Lorraine Rother
Glenna N. Roukes
Edwin & Alice Rounds
Walter L. Rouse
Hamilton Rowan
David & Dian Ruder
Jill M. Rufo
Sandra Ruiz
Ilda Runquist
Albert M. Rush
Mrs. Esther Rush
Ms. Darlene Russ
Mildred A. Russell
Mr. & Mrs. Reeves Russell
Stanley & Lorinda Russell
Patricia A. Shea Ryan
Fred & Ruth Sacher
Mary Ann Sadowski
Herbert H. Saefke
Mr. & Mrs. Byron J. Safstrom
Grace Sagendorf
Evelyn Saintsing
Rev. Jeffrey Samaha
Harry V. Samuelson
Mr. & Mrs. Harry V. Samuelson
Jose Luis Sanchez
David M. Sanders
E. B. Sandler
Howard & Joy Sandlund
Sally Sandoval
E. G. Sandrock
George E. Sanner
Pat Santullo
Helen K. Sapourn
Betty S. Sapp
Nick & Gayle Sarchet
Edward Saroli
Adelia de Yampert Sartor
Mr. & Mrs. Trent Sauder

Ms. Sheri Sauerhoff
Mr. & Mrs. Lowell Savage
Daniel Savlon
Kimberly Sayer
Jim & Yvonne Scabareti
Jim & Donna Scarth
Esther Schaedlich
Marcia K. Schafer
Diane Schaffner
Martha Lou Schakel
Donna L. Schanley
Ruth Scheffler
Betty C. Schemmer
Norman & Helen Schenk
Robert C. Scheyer
Donald & Sue Schieche
Mr. & Mrs. Carl Schiefer
Pastor Albert G. Schiling
Robert L. Schimmel
Mr. & Mrs. Ervin Schmidt
Carl & Elsie Schneider
Harriet Susan Schneider
Orville & Flora Schneider
Terry & Sherry Schneider
Col. & Mrs. William Powers Schneider
Elnora Schnoor
Ellouise Schoenly
Harry & Peggy Schoepp
Ms. Cynthia J. Scholljegerdes
Matt & Ann Scholten
Joseph H. Schoonmaker, M.D.
Clarence Schrader
Cecil Schrock
Dr. Hugo W. Schroeder Sr.
Paul A. Schroeder
Mr. & Mrs. Robert Schuler
Rev. & Mrs. Raymond E. Schultz
Tom Schultz
Mrs. W. E. Schultz (Nadine)
Geoff & Carolyn Schwartz
Mr. & Mrs. Jerry Schwartz
Mr. & Mrs. Paul E. Schwartz
David A. Schwengel
A. Gail Schweyher
Ruth E. Score
Albert Scott
Bill Scott
Clyde & Loretta Scott
H. H. Scott
Kenneth M. Scott, M.D.
Mrs. Elaine Scull
Oliver Sears
Opal A. Sears
Sean R. Sears
Norma J. Seaton
Luella C. Sedivy
Mrs. Alzina Seeley
Donald C. Seest
Clara P. Segevan
Mrs. Edyth Smith Seiple

RONALD B. SELLERS
TIM & LYNN SELLERS
ROELINA SENNESE
SARKIS SEROPIAN
JOSEPH W. SEYFERT
KAREN SHACKELTON
PEGGY & JIM SHACKLEFORD
ADELAIDE SHADDIX
EUNICE W. SHAFFERMAN
FAYE SHARP
MR. JAMES M. SHARP
REV. & MRS. MYRON H. SHARRARD
NORMAN E. SHARRER
DON & ELAINE SHAVER
ELSIE E. SHAW
JANE P. SHAW
MR. & MRS. RICHARD SHEARS
MRS. SARAH S. SHEFFEY
JIM & PAT SHEILS
ELFRIEDA SHELLENBERGER
MICHAEL SHELTON
ROBERTA SHELTON
ALMA JANE SHEPARD
BETH D. SHEPHERD
ROBIN D. SHEPHERD
CHARLES R. SHEPPARD
CLYDE & VERNA SHEPPARD
JANE SHEPPARD
MR. & MRS. EARLL C. SHERIDAN JR.
EARLEEN SHERMAN
RANDY & CHARLOTTE SHERMAN
MS. TAMMIE HILL SHERWOOD
LUCILE SHIDLER
GEORGE W. SHIMER
LYLE L. SHINKLE
MARK J. SHINNERS
MICHAEL & CAROLYN SHIPLEY
RALPH & DEE DEE SHIRLEY
SANOMA SHOFFIT
NELL G. SHORT
HOWARD D. SHOWALTER
MR. & MRS. T. SHOWALTER
MARIE SHRUM
MRS. NAOMI G. SHUMAKER
SCOTT A. SHUMAKER
MARLON SIAS
MRS. ELIZABETH M. SIDES
ED & CLAIRE SIEBERT
MARVIN E. SIEDSCHLAG
ARNOLD SIEG
JIM & SANDIE SIELAFF
MR. & MRS. TIM SIEMENS
JEANETTE SILVER
MR. & MRS. IRVIN SIMMONS
MIKE & ROSE SIMON
M. M. SIMONE
LARRY K. SIMONEAU
HARLEY & GRETTA SIMONSON
JENNIFER L. SIMPSON
BOB & DOT SINGER

MR. & MRS. E. P. SINGLE
MR. & MRS. JONATHAN SITES
EVERETT & ELAINE SJOBERG
MR. & MRS. RONALD SJOSTROM
STEVEN SKALISKY
MR. & MRS. T. F. SKYTTE
ALICE SLAIKEU
TED & PHYLLIS SLAYBAUGH
TOM & REGINA SLOANE
CAROL ANN SLOAT
CHUCK & SHARON SLUSSER
CATHY J. SMELICH
MR. & MRS. ALAN BRESEE SMITH
MRS. AMASA SMITH
MR. & MRS. ANDREW SMITH
ARRETA E. SMITH
MS. BETTY SMITH
CARL DEAN SMITH
CHARLES F. SMITH
E. & LULA SMITH
EDWARD & NATALIE SMITH
MISS ESTHER SMITH
MR. & MRS. GARY W. SMITH
HOMER & GLENNA SMITH
MR. & MRS. JACOB C. SMITH
JACQUELYN SMITH
JOHN & MARY K. SMITH
LEONARD R. SMITH
MRS. MELVIN R. SMITH
REBECCA SMITH
MR. & MRS. RICHARD SMITH
MR. & MRS. ROGER L. SMITH
RUTH P. SMITH
STAN & SHARON SMITH
DR. & MRS. STANLEY T. SMITH JR.
MRS. ARLENE M. SNARE
MR. & MRS. W. L. SNELLGROVE
JAMES W. SNIDER JR.
GINA LYNN SNOW
GLENN & KAMILIA SNYDER
GERALD SOHL
MR. & MRS. RAYMOND L. SOITO
SHARON SOMERS-HILL
MICHELLE M. SORCE
MISS OLGA K. SORENSEN
PATRICIA E. SOUTHWARD
MR. & MRS. ROBERT J. SOUZA
JOY SPACH SMILEY
PAT & NORMA SPARKS
VICTOR & JEANETTE SPENCE
THELMA CROWDER SPENGLER
PHYLLIS SPILLMAN
JIM SPINKS
ADELINE SPRANG
MRS. LILA SPRINGER
FRANCES B. SPRINKLE
JULIA SPRUILL
PETE & JUDY SPULER
JERRY STACKPOLE
REBA STAGGS

PEGGY C. STALA
MS. ELVA STANDS
CHARLES H. STANFORD
EILEEN STANLEY
ROBERT J. STANTON
LEE C. STARE
MR. & MRS. LAVERNE E. STARNER
NANCY R. STARR
WARREN DOYLE STATON SR.
MR. & MRS. EDWARD H. STAUFFER
HOYT A. STEARNS
JEANNE C. STECK
CHERYLL L. STEELE
MRS. GARTH STEELE
MS. RUTH B. STEELE
SUSAN H. STEFFENS
ZOSIA EDWARDS STEGE
MATTIE STEINHAUS
MRS. KAETHE R. STELLA
LESTER STELMA
MR. & MRS. DALE STENBERG
OTTO STENE
MR. & MRS. GORDON STENZEL
MR. & MRS. DENNIS STEPHENS
MR. GERALD V. STEPHENS
IMA JEAN STEPHENS
KATHRYN R. STEPHENS
RANDY STEPHENS
VIRGINIA STEPPLING, R.N.
ELAINE G. STEUERNAGEL
MORRIS L. STEVENS
VIRGINIA M. STEVENSON
MRS. JONAS L. STEWART
VIRGINIA STILL
MR. & MRS. DAN STILLMAN
TEUNIS STOB
BEN STOCKHOLM
KENNA STODDARD
MRS. IRENE STOHL
WILBUR H. STOKES
DR. VERLIN R. STOLLER
NANCY STOLZ
MARY KLING STOLTZFUS
DELORES B. STONE
LAMAR C. STOREY
STORM
MR. & MRS. DAVID L. STORMONT
DON & WANDA STORMS
MR. & MRS. EDWARD P. STOUDENMIRE
MRS. EVE STOUDER
HELEN B. STRADER
MRS. JOHN A. STRAMIELLO
HELEN A. STRAND
MR. & MRS. THEODORE STRATIS
PAT & JACK STRAYER
DAVID & ROMA STREBE
LLOYD & EDNADEAN STRICKLAND
COL. & MRS. C. DAVIS STRIDER
MRS. JOHN R. STROM
CARROLL STROSHINE

MR. & MRS. CLIFFORD D. STRUBHAR
DOUG & HELEN STUBBLEFIELD
HAROLD & DORIS STUDER
DICK & GRETA STUECKLE
ARDA E. STULTS
MR. & MRS. CHARLES D. STULTZ
DORIS I. STUMP
MR. & MRS. LYLE C. STUSEK
DR. & MRS. JOHN SUCHER
JAE RIN SUH
EUGENE & MARY SUKUP
RUTH Q. SULAHIAN
DR. & MRS. CARY E. SULLIVAN
MR. & MRS. STEPHEN N. SUPERITS
DEE SURIANO
MR. & MRS. J. M. SUTTLES
MR. & MRS. CARVER SUTTON
THOMAS J. SWAFFORD JR.
MRS. NANCY L. SWANN
GINNY SWANSON
MR. & MRS. PHILIP A. SWANSON
MR. JACK A. SWARTZENDRUBER
WILLIAM M. SWEET
MR. & MRS. GARY L. SWENSON
CHARLES SWINFORD
ELIZABETH SZWED
MR. R. DUNCAN TAGGART
JAY & ARNISE PEGGY TAKAAZE
DANIEL D. TAMEZ JR., M.D.
ADELINE TAN
FRANK G. TANDY
DEBBY TSENG TANG, PH.D.
MARK D. TANIS
DR. & MRS. HARRY TARPINIAN
SAM C. TATUM
DONALD F. TAUCHER, O.D.
BAILEY & ANN TAYLOR
DORA W. TAYLOR
KATHERINE TAYLOR
ALBERT C. TELLINGTON
REV. CECIL W. TEMPLE
MR. & MRS. W. B. TEMPLE
ROBERT J. TEMPLETON
MR. & MRS. RONALD L. TEN HARMSEL
VINCENT G. TERRY
ALAN & CARROLL TERWILLEGER
CATHIE H. TEW
MOSES & CATHY TEY
MOTHER THERESA, O.C.D.
MARGARET THIEMAN
CHARLOTTE A. THIESSEN
ARTHUR R. THODE JR.
DELAINE & DEB THOMAS
LOWELL V. THOMAS SR.
STEVEN K. THOMAS
CASSIE M. THOMPSON/
DOROTHY G. THOMPSON
JEANNIE & JOE THOMPSON
JOHN & LOUISE THOMPSON
MR. & MRS. KENNETH THOMPSON

DR. & MRS. ROBERT THOMPSON
THEODORE A. THOMPSON
TOM & MARY THOMPSON
MR. & MRS. TRUET B. THOMPSON
THOMPSON'S USED CARS
FRANCES W. THOMSON
REV. & MRS. WILLIAM C. THORE
FAITH & DANNY THORNBURG
REV. DR. LARRY L. THORNTON
MR. & MRS. W. BRIAN THORNTON
HULDA D. THORPE
ANNETTE THORSRUD
MR. & MRS. PETER P. THREE STARS
JIM & DEBBIE TICE
MR. RICHARD TIENHAARA II & MRS.
    ELIZABETH MARTIN-TIENHAARA
ANDY & ELAINE TIESENGA
ALBERT TIKIUN
GORDON & EVELYN TILL
DR. & MRS. WENDELL H. TILLER
RON & CARMEN TIMM
GREG TINKER
MR. & MRS. ANTHONY A. TIONGSON
LEHMEN TIPPIE
MICHAEL PETER TITRE
WALTER F. TITUS
EMILY G. TODD
STEVE & LORRAINE TOGNOLI
PAUL TOKAR
JOHN & SHIRLEY TOLLEFSON
MARVIN V. TORGERSON
DEBORAH M. TORRES
MARIA VICTORIA TORRES
REVA TORREYSON
JOYCE TOW
DORIS TOWNSEND
MR. & MRS. GEORGE TOWNSEND
DONALD L. TRACKWELL
MR. & MRS. VERON H. TRANEL
MR. & MRS. PHIL TRAVIS
EDWARD & VIOLET TREAT
MR. & MRS. JACK C. TRELOAR JR.
DR. & MRS. TODD C. TROLL
JIM & PAM TROMBLEY
MARSHA J. TROSPER
PEGGY TROWBRIDGE
PAUL F. TRUAIR
KATHRYN M. TRUDELL
MR. & MRS. WALTER M. TUCK
CEPHUS TUCKER
DORIS TUINSTRA
MRS. JOHN TULEY
MRS. LOUIS J. TULLIO
LUKE & PAMELA TURCHI
JOHN TURCHINETZ
LAWRENCE F. TURNBULL, M.D.
JOYCE TURNER
MR. & MRS. MALCOLM M. TURNER
SUSAN TURNER
OPAL TUTMARC

Mary Tvarch
Mrs. June Tweed
Esther L. Twigg
Dale & Mary Twining
Stephen Tzeng
Colonel & Mrs. Larry Ullrey
David & Linda Ulmer
Eugene E. Ulmer
Deacon & Carol Umholtz
Mr. & Mrs. Carl W. Umland
Mr. & Mrs. Olaf & Doris Underwood
Mr. & Mrs. Steven P. Undseth
Rose Urdiales-Munoz
Naomi M. Urey
Genevieve J. Utter
Jerrian Van Dellen, M.D.
Mr. & Mrs. Eric A. Van Denhendt
Ginny Van Der Meid
Mr. & Mrs. Robert J. Van Domelen
Mr. & Mrs. Marvin Van Dyk
Mary Van Dyke
Ralph & Gail Van Fossen
Richard D. Van Lunen
John & Ruth Van Patter
Erma L. Van Pool
Mrs. Betty N. Van Slooten
Ms. Corinne E. Van Tol
Arthur R. Van Tuinen
Avis Van Vliet
Harold J. VanCleve
Mr. & Mrs. David L. VanVeld
Robert Vande Bunte
Mr. & Mrs. Richard Vandegrift
Dr. & Mrs. Stanley B. Vander Aarde
Ken & Theresa Vander Kooi
Dan & Becky Vander Meulen
Mr. & Mrs. Donald Vander Schaaf
Mr. & Mrs. John E. Vanderhoff
William S. Vanpatten
Steve & Donna Varnam
C. Lee & Ellen Santilli Vaughn
Mrs. Ruth Vaupel
Dr. & Mrs. Timothy Veenstra
Mr. Gerald P. Vellenga
Linda Vendemo
Dr. & Mrs. Joseph T. Verga
Rich & Mary Verlare
James & Virginia Viani
Steve & Judi Vigh
Walter & Margaret Vikestad
Rev. Bill & Donna Vines
Mr. & Mrs. Eldon E. Virgil
Mrs. Marjorie H. Visser
Albert & Dorothy Vliem
Gordon & Verla Voght
Dr. & Mrs. Vernon Vogt
Mr. & Mrs. Steve Voisard
Mr. & Mrs. J. Stanley Vollmert
Peter & Marian Voltman
Mrs. Edwin E. Vonada

Craig Voorhees
George & Friedel Votava
Edna & Neil Voth
Ron Vought
Mrs. Henry Wacker
Rev. & Mrs. Yasushi D. Wada
Mr. & Mrs. Douglas C. Wade
Dick & Becky Wagler
Mrs. Glenn Wagoner
Leonard & Eileen Wahlberg
Naomi Waibel
Bill & Rita Wainscott
John Walheim
Mr. & Mrs. Herman Walker
Mr. & Mrs. Max Walker
Thomas M. Walker
Prof. & Mrs. William D. Walker
Richard & Jean Wall
Terry & Karen Wall
Ella Ruth Wallace
Emmett A. Wallace
Mrs. Linda S. Wallace
Mr. & Mrs. Mark Wallace
R. Carol Wallenstein
Don & Trudy Walley
Jane & Craig Walliker
Phyllis Walmsley
Mr. & Mrs. James P. Walsh
Robert & Sloan Walsh
Randall Walters
Hazel M. Wampler
Steve Warcham
Dalton & Marjory Ward
Ray & Linda Ward
Ruth E. Wardell
Gary & Pam Ware
Barbara & Richard Warner
Harriet Warner
Norma A. Warner
Dorothy C. Warnock
Bob & Nancy Warren
Mrs. Stanley Washburn
David D. Wasson
Joanne Waters
Alberta Watson
C. S. Watson
Elizabeth A. Watson
Jonathan Watson
Mr. & Mrs. Richard Watts
Lori Ann R. Waye
Alvin M. Weaver
Danny C. Weaver
Mr. & Mrs. Richard L. Weaver
Dale & Janice Webb
Linda Benfatto Weber
Mr. & Mrs. Richard L. Weber
Mr. & Mrs. William F. Weber
Mrs. D. D. Webster
Leo A. Wehner
Mr. & Mrs. Earl Weirich

Morgan & JoAnn Weistling & Family
Rev. & Mrs. Lester R. Weko
Ricky Welborn
Mrs. W. W. Welch
Richard & Virginia Wellock
David & Tammy Wells
Dr. & Mrs Donald W. Wells
Jean & Gordon Wells
Charles Welsh
Dr. Norma R. Wendelburg
Herbert H. Wendell
Mr. & Mrs. John Wennblom
Mr. & Mrs. Vincent G. Wessel
Norma C. Wessner
Joan West
Marsha West
Sueann J. West
Mrs. Leona H. Westerdahl
Elsie Westra
Frances W. Wetherwax
Mr. & Mrs. C. Davis Weyerhaeuser
Mr. & Mrs. Larry C. Wheatley
Edgar F. Wheeler
Abner & Pauline White
Colbert W. F. White
Mr. & Mrs. E. M. White
Gary White
Janice R. White
Mr. & Mrs. Kenneth White
Lucy Constance White
Miss Mattie White
Patricia South White
Ralph & Phyllis White
Terry & Sharon White
William L. White, M.D.
Gladys Whiteside
Mrs. Nancy L. Whiting
Mr. & Mrs. Stephen Whiton
David S. Whittaker
Ransom A. (Randy) Whittle
Hugh C. Whyte
Mr. & Mrs. Lynn Widger
Mrs. Loraine P. Widman
Alfred H. Wiebe
Leonard Wiebe
Arthur L. Wieberdink
Dr. & Mrs. Alvin Wiens
Elizabeth G. Wiens
Mary A. Wientjes
Tom & Deb Wier
Henry E. & Theresa Wiers
Mary J. Wilber
Juanita Wilburn
Veda Wilburn
Pat Wilcox
Bill & Carol Wilder
Malcolm G. Wilkes
Mary Wilkes
Mr. & Mrs. Mark S. Wilkins
Dale L. Wilkinson

Thelma Willard
Mr. & Mrs. Stanley Wille
Christopher S. Williams
Dan & Vicki Williams
Evelyn R. Williams
Dr. & Mrs. Francis J. Williams
Gordon & Edie Williams
Mr. M. E. Williams
Mr. & Mrs. Michael S. Williams
Franklin E. Williamson
Mr. & Mrs. Henry G. Wills
Al & Lellan Wilson
Mrs. Elizabeth Wilson
Mr. & Mrs. M. W. Wilson
Mr. Ronald G. Wilson
Waldo W. Wilson Jr.
Marguerite Wilt
Dr. Bonnie c. Wimberly
Mr. & Mrs. David W. Windatt
Patty Ford Windsor
Debra Winger
Todd & Robin Winkler
Christine Winstead
Birger & Marianne Wiresee
Irene Wisniewski
Mrs. A. M. Withers
J. Gregory Witt
Mrs. Gwendolene R. Wittmann
Gene Wohlberg
Larry & Sheila Wolf
Mr. & Mrs. Robert C. Wolfe
Cindy Wolff
Ivey C. Wolpert
Herman & Bee Wolter
Phillip & Betty Wolz
Mr. Todd Womack
Frank & Anne Wonder
Dick Wong
Dr. & Mrs. Chongkyoo Woo
Mrs. Billy C. Wood
Joanna Glassell Wood
Helen Wood Wyrosdick
Becky & George Woodin
Ruth Anne Woodman
Mrs. Howell D. Woodson
Brenda Woody
Joseph & Thelma Woody
Mrs. Joyce E. Woolsey
Frank & Irene Wordhouse
John Workman
Dennie & Loretta Worthington
Doris K. Wottrich
Mary C. Wray
Sue Wrhen
The Wright Family
Barbara M. Wright
Craig L. Wright
Frances I. Wright
Mr. & Mrs. John P. Wright
Mr. Malcolm Wright

T. J. & Bonnie Wright
Tom & Dawn Wright
Walter W. Wright
Charles A. Wulf III
Robert M. Wunderlich
Mr. & Mrs. Edward S. Wyatt
April Yearick
Liv A. Yeaworth
Margaret Yelland
Dr. & Mrs. J. Thomas Ylvisaker
Mr. & Mrs. Charles D. Yoder
Joseph Yoder
Magdalena Yoder
Wayne & Claudia York
Ms. Caryn Yost
Cathreyn D. Young
Charles Young
Dr. & Mrs. Charles R. Young
J. M. Young
Marion J. Young Jr.
Nancy L. Young
Roland & Martha Young
Dwight & Kathy Youngberg
Greg & Emily Yoxsimer
Maria & Kwang S. Yum
Mr. & Mrs. Jeffrey Yunginger
Jim & Letha Zahourek
Mr. & Mrs. David L. Zarri
Wallace & Cynthia Zellmer
Gundega Zemzars
Ardys E. Zetter
Sarah C. Zick
Douglas E. Ziel
Mr. William Zilisch
Mary L. Zilz
Ms. Elsie Zimmerman
Mert & Donna Zimmerman
Tricia Zimmerman
Kenneth Zmuda
Eleanor Zoellick
Omar Zook Jr.
Paul E. Zumbrun

BERTHA FISCHER . . . . RICHARD E. COLEMAN
DR. IRIS C. FISCHER . . . . MS. LUCY G. RODMAN
NEIL EDWARD FISH . . . . V. SHIRLEY FISH
RON FISHER . . . . JIM SPINKS
ORLONZO FLANDERS . . . . MRS. ORLONZO FLANDERS
DAVE FORD & SHELLEY FORD
   VASQUEZ . . . . PATTY FORD WINDSOR
MISS MELODY FORNEY . . . . MISS CARY A. CARTER
DR. JAMES FORRESTER . . . . DOROTHY JUDY
REV. DWIGHT FOSTER . . . . MR. RONALD G. WILSON
BRO. FRANK . . . . FRANKLIN E. WILLIAMSON
MILDRED E. FRANZE . . . . ANONYMOUS
DONALD FREAM . . . . MRS. DONALD FREAM
PAULINE A. FREDERICK . . . . MR. GROVER FREDERICK
MARNIE FREDERICKSON . . . . VERNON W. FREDERICKSON
GEORGE B. FREEMAN . . . . ELISE W. FREEMAN
MR. & MRS. JAMES D. FREEMAN . . . . MR. & MRS. JAMES R. FREEMAN
DIANE FRIEND . . . . KARINE MATTER
HAROLD FRITZ . . . . MRS. SHIRLEY FRITZ
ELLEN FRITZLAN . . . . LESLIE C. FRITZLAN
JUANITA M. FROHM . . . . JOAN M. REYNOLDS
GEARY & FLORENCE FULLER . . . . . . MR. RONALD PAGANO-FULLER
ALBERT R. GANN . . . . VIRGINIA GANN
ARTHUR GANNON . . . . ARTHUR GANNON
MARTHA E. GARRETT . . . . MR. & MRS. GENE L. MAHN
HEATHER GAUME . . . . MRS. AMOS GAUME
DIANA GENDRY . . . . MAXINE REESER
IRENE SLATER GERMER . . . . MRS. MIMI GERMER
HELEN GILBERT . . . . JEAN W. KOUBA
MELVIA GILES . . . . MELVIA GILES
FRED GILREATH . . . . PAUL & FRAN MORABITH
ARLENE D. GLANCE . . . . JOHN C. GLANCE
JENNIFER GRIST GOODIN . . . . WANDA G. GILCHRIST
OLEN GORBY . . . . GINNY VAN DER MEID
LEWIS H. GOULD JR. . . . . MARGUERITE GOULD
ADA MAE GRAHAM . . . . MILDRED L. GRAHAM
DR. REVEREND BILLY GRAHAM . . . . REV. & MRS. HERMAN D. GERRISH
REV. BRIAN GRAHAM . . . . DEBBIE FOWLER
DOROTHY M. GRAYBILL . . . . ANNA J. GRAYBILL
MR. ODELL GREGORY . . . . ROBIN & ALLEN LANKFORD
LOUISE GRESHAM . . . . JULIAN GRESHAM
MRS. SUSAN P. GROSSE . . . . SHERRY D. GROSSE
JOHN & CONNIE GROSSKREUTZ . . . . CONNIE HIPPLE
ALFRED CARMON GROUNDS . . . . . . MRS. KATIE M. GROUNDS
JACK J. GUNTHER . . . . MR. & MRS. JIM GUNTHER
PETER F. GUNTHER . . . . PHYLLIS J. GUNTHER
LYNNETTE GUSTAFSON . . . . MS. JUNE GUSTAFSON
JERRY HAADSMA . . . . ROBERT & CORRIE DECKER
MRS. B. J. HAAN . . . . MRS. B. J. HAAN
GLADYS HADLEY . . . . GORDON HADLEY
DONALD C. HAESLOOP . . . . MRS. BETTY C. HAESLOOP
HARRY C. HAGEY . . . . MABEL E. HAGEY
JACK HALFEN . . . . MAYNARD "KNUTE" KNUTSON
JOHN W. HAMILTON SR. . . . . RONALD T. HAMILTON, D.M.D.
MR. & MRS. ANDREW G. HANNERS . . MR. & MRS. LOREN C. GROSSI
EDWARD H. HARDEN . . . . BARBARA BIER
JOHNNIE F. HARELSON . . . . WILLIAM F. HARELSON
ANNE M. HAROUN . . . . NAJI HAROUN
ALONZO HARRIS . . . . ULI CHAPA
ELAINE HARRIS . . . . VERNON C. HARRIS

WADE H. HARRIS . . . . HOYT A. STEARNS
DAVID R. HART . . . . LU ELLA J. HART
HEIDI HARTFORD . . . . JOHN HARTFORD
ALTON C. HARTSELL . . . . DOLORES R. HARTSELL
RUTH HEASLEY . . . . DAWN E. CRISE
ERNEST P. HEBERT SR. . . . . MR. & MRS. ERNEST P. HERBERT JR.
MS. MICHELLE LOUISE HENDY . . . . MR. GARY LEE CLAYTON
VIOLET L. HENNING . . . . ROBERT C. HENNING
LORA E. HERMISTONE . . . . JOHN HERMISTONE
TONY HERNANDEZ . . . . SERGIO & MARIA HERNANDEZ
HAROLD F. HERNDON . . . . MRS. LOLA HERNDON
HARVEY J. HESS JR. . . . . ESTHER HESS
SEAN L. HESS . . . . HELEN M. HESS
RICHARD HETTINGA . . . . LORI L. KECK
DAVID A. HICKEY . . . . ISABEL COUSTEN
CARL J. HOCH . . . . MRS. BETTY JOHNSON
WILLIS E. HODGMAN . . . . DR. KATHLEEN A. HODGMAN
SHIRLEY & WALTER HUFF . . . . TURNER & GRETCHEN BAKER
ANNABELLE DODGE HUGHES . . . . . ANNE V. FURNO
MRS. FRANCES HUGHES . . . . MR. & MRS. DALE GREER
EUGENE CHARLES HUGUNIN . . . . . DORIS M. HUGUNIN
MR. JOHN T. HULTGREN . . . . MRS. JOHN T. HULTGREN
MONA HUNT . . . . ANNIE W. HOWARD, LEON &
                                       MILLIE GIRDNER
EDMAE MARIE HUNTER . . . . MARCIA J. HUNTER
WESLEY R. HURST . . . . MRS. WESLEY R. HURST
PASTOR WILLIAM L. HURST . . . . . . WILLIAM LEE PHIPPS
MRS. EDITH C. HUTCHINSON . . . . . MR. & MRS. ROBERT KENNEDY
JAMES HUTCHISON . . . . JENNIFER J. BOCK
EARL E. IRVINE . . . . VIRGINIA L. IRVINE
THOMAS WARDELL IVERY JR. . . . . . JEAN MARIE IVERY
DEE DEE JACKSON . . . . CHARLES E. JACKSON
KENNETH JACKSON . . . . ANDREW NEITA
STEPHANIE E. JACKSON . . . . BETTY R. FOX
AVA JAMES . . . . PAUL S. JAMES
CARL V. JAMES . . . . LUCILLE A. JAMES
CHAD ELLIOT JAMES . . . . SANDRA JAMES
REV. W. B. JAMISON . . . . DR. & MRS. PAUL W. JAMISON
REV. & MRS. PHILIP JAQUITH . . . . . MRS. DOT M. LIS
STAN & JANIS JARRETT . . . . STEVE & DONNA VARNAM
ARTHUR JEETER . . . . ESTHER R. BOWMAN
MR. ALBERT JUNIOR JENKINS . . . . . MISS DIANNE JENKINS
DELMA JENKINS . . . . MRS. ARTHUR ALLAIRE
CHESTER H. JENNINGS . . . . LEILA & DON LANDGREBE
HAROLD E. JENSEN . . . . MR. HAROLD J. JENSEN
JESUS CHRIST, SAVIOR . . . . SEVERAL ANNIVERSARY PARTNERS
EARL C. JOBE . . . . CLARA C. JOBE
DISCIPLE JOHN, FATHER ABRAHAM,
   MOSES . . . . MR. ELTON L. HOPKINS
ARCHIE L. JOHNSON . . . . ARLENE L. JOHNSON
ARDEN JOHNSON . . . . RUSS & LOIS JOHNSON
BLAKE JOHNSON . . . . KENNA STODDARD
DAVID H. R. JOHNSON . . . . JUDITH C. JOHNSON
JUDGE DON JOHNSON . . . . ANONYMOUS
MR. & MRS. LAWRENCE A. JOHNSON . MRS. RUTH JOHNSON
WILLIAM P. JOHNSON . . . . THAD P. JOHNSON
JUDGE JOE M. JOINER . . . . STEVE & JENNIE CARRELL
MR. & MRS. GEORGE H. JONES . . . . RALPH & MARGE LLOYD
JAMES L. JONES . . . . MISS ROBERTA E. JONES
DR. ROBERT F. JONES . . . . MRS. ROBERT F. JONES

JESS P. JORDAN SR. . . . . MRS. MARGARET JORDAN
MR. & MRS. LEWIS JORDAN . . . . . . BETTY L. JORDAN
R. H. JOYNT . . . . M. C. JOYNT
EPPA D. KANE . . . . MS. JEAN MURPHY
JOLEY KARNIG . . . . GARY KARNIG
MIRIAM & REINO KARY . . . . JAN KARY
G. EILEEN KATS . . . . EDWARD I. KATS
PAUL H. KATS . . . . HAROLD J. KATS
MR. & MRS. W. C. KENTZEL SR. . . . . RUTH P. KENTZEL
PHYLLIS ANN KIK . . . . DR. FRANK N. KIK
TOM KILLEY . . . . ROBERT M. PETERHANS
MARY ANNETTE KINKAID . . . . NASON E. KINKAID
MR. & MRS. JERRY KIRK . . . . ANONYMOUS
GENE KITTERMAN . . . . CHRIS KITTERMAN
BLAINE F. KNEEBONE . . . . LEAH D. KNEEBONE
NANCY ANN KOHLMAN . . . . LOU KOHLMAN
MILDRED KRANICK . . . . MR. & MRS. TIMOTHY J. KRANICK
LLOYD FRANK KRUEGER . . . . DAVID L. KRUEGER SR.
PAUL M. KUCK . . . . WALLACE & MARIAN KUCK
MR. & MRS. FIL KYLLINGMARK . . . . MR. & MRS. T. F. SKYTTE
DANIEL Y. LAM . . . . MRS. DANIEL LAM
THOMAS F. LANIER . . . . MARILYN LANIER
PHILIP E. LARSON . . . . LOUANN LARSON
JOHN LATONA . . . . CHRIS A. NEAL
BRIAN LAUDENBACK . . . . DR. RICHARD E. CRAMM
JAN DAVIS LAYTON . . . . MISS MARY H. DAVIS
TODD LUCIEN LEBLANC . . . . DONALD L. LEBLANC
SIDNEY A. LEE . . . . MRS. FRANKIE M. LEE
MRS. LORETTA LEEF . . . . MR. & MRS. B. R. JOHNSON
MRS. AMELIA N. LEHMANN . . . . . . MR. & MRS. VINCENT G. WESSEL
MARY LOU LEICHTY . . . . DANNY & CAROL LEICHTY
REVEREND MILTON K. LEIDIG . . . . . LOIS J. LEIDIG
ROSELLEN D. LEWIS . . . . C. GORDON LEWIS
MR. LEWIS LINE . . . . MR. & MRS. LA VERNE E. STARNER
LAVON P. LINN . . . . RUBY WINSLOW LINN
QUEEN J. LOBDELL . . . . MRS. GWENDOLENE R. WITTMANN
MR. COYTE LOCKEE SR. . . . . MRS. BETTY LOCKEE
ROBERT ALTON LONG . . . . ROBERT ALTON LONG
JEAN LORENZO . . . . MS. DOLORES LORENZO
HERBERT LOTTER . . . . RACHEL LOTTER
FAYETTA LOWELL . . . . MRS. JOHN TULEY
DAVID LEE LUPER . . . . MR. & MRS. FRED D. LUPER
ERIK L. LUTTON . . . . DONALD LUTTON, D.V.M.
MARK H. LUTTRELL . . . . REV. & MRS. ELEE HYDEN
WILLIAM T. LYMAN . . . . HELEN T. LYMAN
JAMES LYNCH . . . . ED & CLAIRE SIEBERT
MRS. ELSIE MAY LYONS . . . . DEFORD L. LYONS
WILLIAM K. LYONS . . . . CASSIE M. THOMPSON
PHILIP M. LYTLE . . . . EMILY G. LYTLE
HELEN MAAHS . . . . ED & SANDRA POOCK
ROYCE L. MAGNUSON . . . . M. BETTY MAGNUSON
REV. O. VICTOR MAGNUSSEN . . . . . ESTHER MAGNUSSEN
PATRICIA MAHOOD . . . . KENNETH & HELEN MAHOOD
ROBERT JAMES MANDARINO . . . . . PETER & KATHRYN MANDARINO
BARRY D. MARCHINKOSKI . . . . . . DR. & MRS. J. GREGORY JAVORNISKY
HARRY MARKUS . . . . BARBARA MARKUS
HELEN MARIE MARRS . . . . MR. & MRS. W. D. MARRS
CLARA A. MARTIN . . . . MICHAEL & SANDRA MARTIN
MICHAEL MARTINEZ . . . . REV. JEFFREY SAMAHA
MARY . . . . L. NESBITT

Francis (Frank) Snare ....Mrs. Arlene M. Snare
James W. Snider Sr. ....James W. Snider Jr.
Bob Snow ....Gina Lynn Snow
Mary Carol Spanski ....Mary A. Wientjes
Marica St. Clair ....Cephus Tucker
Ronald St. Laurent ....Ms. Sheri Sauerhoff
Neal Stands ....Ms. Elva Stands
William Stanley ....Eileen Stanley
Audrey F. Stanton ....Robert J. Stanton
Leroy Staymates ....Karen Staymates Kallenborn
Douglas A. Steele ....Ms. Ruth B. Steele
Daniel F. Stella ....Mrs. Kaethe R. Stella
Ben Stephenson ....Al & Mary Jo Bonds
Oscar H. Steuernagel ....Elaine G. Steuernagel
Ross & Ruth Stevens ....Flip & Marguerite Felton
Robert & Viola Stewart ......Mr. & Mrs. Edwin Kessler
Emilie Stockholm ....Ben Stockholm
Paul Stolz ....Nancy Stolz
Mr. John A. Stramiello ......Mrs. John A. Stramiello
John R. Strom ....Mrs. John R. Strom
Annie Mae Stromberg ....Mrs. Dorothy D. Roper
Maxine Stroshine ....Carroll Stroshine
Gerald Stump ....Doris I. Stump
Joni A. Stump ....Anonymous
James B. Sullivan II ....Shirley M. Mercurio
Craig M. Szwed ....Elizabeth Szwed
Joni Eareckson Tada ....Randy & Charlotte Sherman
Helen Spruce Tampke ....Bill & Lillian Nogues
Ida G. Tandy ....Frank G. Tandy
Vera Eve Tate ....Robert E. Heath
Athol Lee Taylor ....Bailey & Ann Taylor
Donn Tee ....Mr. & Mrs. F. Laurence Gosnell
Mother Teresa ....Mr. & Mrs. Herbert A. Gardner Jr.
George & Kathryn Terwilleger .Alan & Carroll Terwilleger
Della C. Goff Thomas ....Lowell V. Thomas Sr.
Amy Julia Thompson ....Thompson's Used Cars
Mr. W. Ralph Thompson ......Anonymous
Lewie & Martha Tidwell ......Steve & Donna Varnam
Nick Timko ....Ken & Patricia Miller
Bernard Timmerman ....Mr. & Mrs. Roger A. DeHaan
Jed Anthony Babanto Torres ...Deborah M. Torres
Rommel S. Torres ....Maria Victoria Torres
Emma Tow ....Joyce Tow
Betty Trombley ....Jim & Pam Trombley
Richard P. Trudell ....Kathryn M. Trudell
Robert J. Tuinstra ....Doris Tuinstra
Owen Turner ....Eleanor Zoellick
Dennis & Louise Twigg ....Esther L. Twigg
Marian Tzeng ....Stephen Tzeng
Mrs. Marjorie Van Buren ......Miss Lucile Lukens
Kenneth Van Dellen ....Jerrian Van Dellen, M.D.
Mr. & Mrs. Marvin Van Dyk ...Mr. & Mrs. Marvin Van Dyk
Rev. Clarence Van Slooten ....Mrs. Betty N. Van Slooten
William A. Van Tol ....Ms. Corinne E. Van Tol
Mabel Van Witt ....Mary Jane Billingsley
Molly Voss ....Peggy King
Alex Waibel ....Naomi Waibel
R. C. Walker Sr. ....Christopher R. Boyd
Harold S. Wallace ....Ella Ruth Wallace
Wesley A. Walters ....Janet L. McCutchen

Lorraine C. Wardell ....Ruth E. Wardell
Thomas Warren Jr. ....Leasteen H. Hamilton
Pastor Stanley Washburn ....Mrs. Stanley Washburn
Laura I. Watson ....Rev. C. E. Brentlinger
Philip E. Watts ....Mr. & Mrs. Richard Watts
A. L. Weber ....Mr. & Mrs. Harold D. Brenneke
Leslie Wells Jr. ....Ann Rice Parsons
Mrs. Anna L. Wendelburg ......Dr. Norma R. Wendelburg
Kenneth T. Wessner ....Norma C. Wessner
Byron West ....Marsha West
Nolan West ....Ouida Gray
John H. Westerland ....Virginia Rodner Abbitt
John H. Westra ....Elsie Westra
Mr. Charles Wheatley ....Mr. & Mrs. Larry C. Wheatley
Holly White ....Colbert W. F. White
Ralf & Carol White ....Steve & Donna Varnam
Terry White ....James W. Greig
Florence Whiting ....Barry Nilson & Laura Livingston
Mrs. Doris E. Whyte ....Hugh C. Whyte
Mr. Lee E. Widman ....Mrs. Loraine P. Widman
Georgia N. Wild ....Sharon Fetters
Ann Ekings Williams ....Mr. M. E. Williams
Tene Malika Williams ....Christopher S. Williams
Ruby G. Wills ....Mr. & Mrs. Henry G. Wills
Paul & Patty Willyard ....June Kemalyan
Mr. Harry Wilson ....Mrs. Elizabeth Wilson
Ronald Paul Wilson ....Mr. & Mrs. M. W. Wilson
Rosa Hardison Winfree ....Dora W. Taylor
Michael L. Winger ....Debra Winger
Marlyn Witmer ....Sharon Abendschoen
Terry & Nancy Womack ....Mr. Todd Womack
Nancy A. Woods ....Lucille P. Collins
John Reid Woodward ....Andrena & Donald F. Phillips
Mrs. Larry L. Wray ....God's Love Ministries
Andrew J. Wright ....Mr. Malcolm Wright
Cynthia Wunderlich ....Robert M. Wunderlich
Rev. & Mrs. Lyle York ....Rev. & Mrs. Daniel D. DeJesus
Richard A. Yost ....Ms. Caryn Yost
Charlie Young ....Mr. & Mrs. Robert J. Souza
Johanna M. Young ....J. M. Young
Youth to Youth Catholic
    Evangelization ....Luke & Pamela Turchi
Linda A. Zarri ....Mr. & Mrs. David L. Zarri
Evelyn M. Zumbrun ....Paul E. Zumbrun